Wicked
ERIE

JUSTIN DOMBROWSKI

THE
History
PRESS

Published by The History Press
Charleston, SC
www.historypress.com

Cover images are used with permission from the Erie County Historical Society and the Pennsylvania State Archives.

First published 2023

Manufactured in the United States

ISBN 9781467155311

Library of Congress Control Number: 2023938572

Notice: The information in this book is true and complete to the best of our knowledge. It is offered without guarantee on the part of the author or The History Press. The author and The History Press disclaim all liability in connection with the use of this book.

Hell is empty and all the devils are here.
—*William Shakespeare*

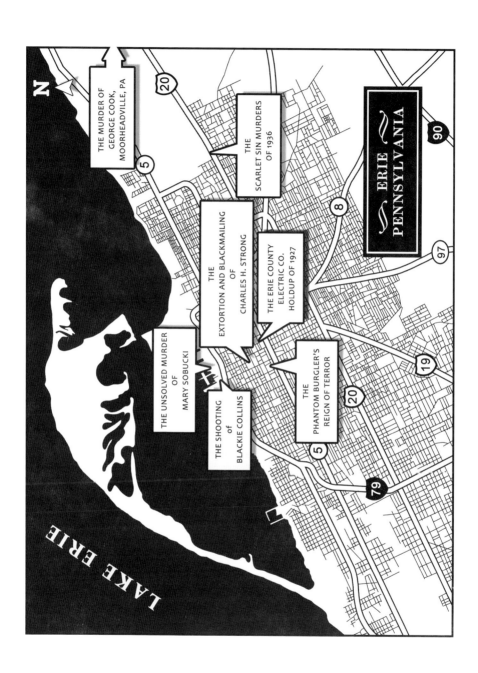

CONTENTS

ACKNOWLEDGEMENTS

Crafting this book was both enigmatic and challenging. Without the support of many individuals, this book could not have been possible. My managing editor, J. Banks Smither, provided endless support, jumping through many hurdles to help make *Wicked Erie* a reality.

The staff of the Lawrence History Center in Lawrence, Massachusetts, went above and beyond with numerous inquiries and emails when researching Joseph "Blackie" Collins, a Lawrence native. Their assistance helped in separating fact from fiction regarding sensational news articles from 1908.

Nancy Uffindell and the Friends of Mount Hope Cemetery in Rochester, New York, provided burial documentation about the family of Ferdinand Fischer and helped corroborate information that helped confirm the whereabouts of Fischer after he vanished from the State Hospital for the Insane in Warren, Pennsylvania. Pennsylvania State Archives staff also provided crucial medical records related to Fischer's admittance at the state hospital from 1908 to 1911.

The Erie County Historical Society, as it has in the past, provided its support from the beginning. Despite historical true crime being a hotly debated topic in relation to general history, Cal Pifer and his staff continue to support local historians.

Jerry Skrypzak, who has been a wealth of knowledge on Erie history, located the photograph of the old Erie County Jail, published here for the first time.

Dave Lindgren was kind enough to reach out and provide information about his ancestor Ferdinand Fischer. Some of Dave's information helped confirm some of the details of Ferdinand Fischer's life.

My father, Gary Dombrowski, helped again with the maps in this book. Both he and my mother remain my biggest supporters.

Historical true crime often walks a fine line between passion and obsession. I've been grateful throughout this journey to have friends and family who support me. This includes the support and love of my wife and children, who continue to inspire me and remind me that all is possible with a little patience, love and faith.

INTRODUCTION

*W*hat does it mean to be wicked?
Is it callous murder?
Committing a sin against God?
Some say to be wicked is to be black-hearted or corrupt in nature.

Erie, Pennsylvania, has had its fair share of wickedness, especially since European settlers first arrived in the region in 1753. Although one would be uninformed of the deranged and macabre history forever steeped in the city's soil.

Harking back on the past, some say the term *wicked* is insufficient.

Despite the Gem City being the fifth-largest city in Pennsylvania, its crimes rival those of the nearby cities of Buffalo, Cleveland and Pittsburgh.

The seven stories scribed on the sheets that follow are those long forgotten, with narratives of an iniquitous nature, painstakingly researched and visualized for the first time in almost a decade. These stories allow us to once again revisit the cold, darkened streets and back alleyways from long ago.

The Gem City continues to reveal its secrets from history.

The research for these cases was pulled from cases within archival records for the Court of Oyer and Terminer of Erie County, which span from 1823 to the early 1950s. These records, on permanent loan from Erie County, contributed many details that are being released for the first time.

When Ferdinand Fischer escaped from the State Hospital for the Insane in Warren in August 1911, he vanished and was never apprehended. A substantial number of newspaper articles and Fischer's case file aided in the discovery of Fischer's whereabouts nearly 112 years after he disappeared in an dramatic case that haunted law enforcement well into the 1940s.

After Samuel Weed was hospitalized following the murder of his family (Erie's first recorded mass murder), the survival of his patient history records provided an astonishing insight into Weed's mental instability. These records, never publicly revealed, divulged yet another tragic angle of the case.

Ninety-six years after the murderous Phantom Burglar terrorized the city of Erie in January 1926, research, assisted by the inclusion of criminal profiling, has brought us one step closer to revealing his identity.

Other cases plunge beyond the boundaries of the partitions of Erie's black-and-white headlines. With its fair share of research came numerous roadblocks and dead ends. The individuals who are forever intertwined with these crimes are long deceased. Original records have either been lost or destroyed. Much of the landscape of Old Erie has been eradicated by modernization and technology.

What remains is a once buried past, flourishing with tragedy, triumph and loss, reaching out beyond the sensational headlines and gory details that once quenched the insatiable hunger of thousands. For the victims and their families, whose lives remain altered, this book serves as a bookend to such legacies, in that their struggles and forfeiture should never be forgotten. "The belief in a supernatural source of evil is not necessary," wrote famed author Joseph Conrad. "Men alone are quite capable of every wickedness."

1

"DANCE! DANCE, I TELL YOU!"

Blackie Collins and the Suicide of Edward "Erie Slim" Acheson

D ark clouds whisked over the horizon of Presque Isle Bay, whose frigid, choppy, tempestuous waves crashed against the shoreline on the afternoon of February 27, 1908. Ships and freighters idled closely together in the numerous slips and basins on the shore, rolling back and forth against the waters as snow flurries trickled from an impending ceiling of obscurity from above, threatening to devour the city.

The distinguishable sounds of the wharfs, fisheries and factories sputtering to life, visible through plumes of black smoke on the bayfront, could be heard.

At the foot of Sassafras Street, north of a pair of railroad tracks belonging to the Pennsylvania Railroad, was the colossal, two-story brick retort house of the Erie Gas Company. The southern portion of the retort house comprised a large, floorless room that accommodated enormous piles of coal and coke. To the north, the building was divided into two floors, accessible by a narrow stairwell leading to the second floor, where firemen tended to the furnaces. The pungent emanation of coal and natural gas permeated the second floor that afternoon as a lone firemen fed the furnaces.

Soon, transients meandered to the retort house, seeking immediate sanctuary from the weather, huddling near the heat that discharged from the furnaces. The room itself was also littered with trash and covered in a thick layer of black soot.

The conditions were not lost on the transients, thrown into a life of squalor and penury.

Grounds of the Erie Gas Company property showing conditions similar to those of February 1908. Note the USS *Wolverine*. *From the Erie County Historical Society.*

The congregation of transients within the retort house, however, was not without controversy, as this often turned the structure into the site of brawls between rival transient gang members. In time, the criminal activities attracted the attention of Edward Wagner, the police chief for the City of Erie Police Department.

Chief Wagner warned the night watchman at the gas company that the transients should be forbidden from gathering there. Trouble would undoubtedly follow, he warned.

Wagner's foreboding would prove to be calamitous.

Outside the brick walls of the retort house, the howling wind was drowned out by an atmosphere variegated by howling laughter, jaunty melodies and inconsequential conversations among the thirty-plus transients, their identities barely perceptible amid a thick layer of smoke that distorted their shadows cast by the flickering fires nearby.

On a bench east of the furnaces sat a half-dozen transients. One of them was a man known as "Blackie" Collins. Soon, the men were greeted by another passing transient, "Erie Slim," who weaved among the groups

An aerial view of Erie's bayfront. Note the tall smokestack and portions of the old retort house. *From the Erie County Historical Society.*

of men, exchanging pleasantries with Collins before joining another group close by.

Soon, a whiskey bottle appeared and was passed around the men. Collins clutched the bottle, taking a drawn-out swig.

"Here, damn you, leave some for somebody else!" Erie Slim cried out.

Collins lowered the bottle from his mouth, concealing it behind his back. "What in the hell have you got to say about it? I don't see you coughing up anything for the bunch around here."

As Collins handed the bottle off to someone else, Acheson rose and broke into a fiery tirade directed at Collins.

"Fade away," Collins scoffed, waving his hand.

What followed was a vigorous exchange of vile epithets between both men as nearby voices became muted. Acheson stepped up to Collins, only to be thrown onto the bench Collins had been sitting on.

"You behave yourself, or I'll put a crimp in you you won't be likely to forget," Collins squawked at Acheson. "I can lick you or any of your gang, and I don't have to accept your company if I don't want to, see?"

Acheson, slow to his feet, looked around the room, clearly humiliated by Collins. "I'll get an iron and knock your damn block off, you bastard!" Acheson seethed as he stepped toward Collins.

Both men were immediately separated by their respective groups of acquaintances, who sought to quell the rising tension.

"I'll kill you!" Acheson grumbled before leaving the room.

Collins took his seat on the bench with those around him.

"You don't want to be caught napping by Slim." they warned.

Collins brushed off the warning with a chuckle, and soon, the jovial gossip returned, with the scuffle between both men becoming a bygone memory. An hour later, Acheson reappeared, his hands hidden within the pockets of his overcoat.

"Are you as good a man as you were when I was here before?" Acheson called out.

"Yes, I'm as good a man now as I was then," Collins responded curtly.

Acheson approached Collins, extracting a .32-caliber revolver from his pocket. Those near Acheson stumbled backward with vigilance, as the only sound in the room came from the crackling furnaces.

Collins remained unfazed at the sight of Acheson's revolver.

"I don't have to dance for you or any other man," Collins replied, standing up.

"Dance, you bastard, or I'll turn you into a human sieve!" Acheson bellowed with a swelling rage.

Collins ignored Acheson as he pulled back the hammer of his revolver.

"Dance!" Acheson growled, again. "Dance, I tell you!"

Sparse banter from those around was quenched when the room was instantaneously filled with the ear-splitting bark of Acheson's revolver, the bullet ripping through the air and striking the brick wall above Collins's head.

Collins lunged at Acheson, and the two became ensnared in a fight of life or death. As they fell to the ground, Acheson rammed the muzzle of his revolver against Collin and pulled the trigger again. Collins's eyes widened as his grip on Acheson loosened.

Acheson jumped to his feet as Collins's body rolled to the ground against a pile of coal. Turning to the men behind him, Acheson lifted the revolver again, his mouth trembling with fear, having realized what he had done.

"Don't any of you guys make a move, or I'll blow your damn heads off!" Acheson wailed, inching toward the stairwell, his only means of escape. "Get back, or I'll send you all to hell!"

Some of the men appeared as if they would try to seize Acheson, causing him to pull the hammer back on his revolver.

"Don't any of you try to follow me, or this place will hold some more dead men," Acheson warned.

Promptly, Acheson sprinted through the doorway of the stairwell and disappeared. Out of fear, those who remained in the retort house fled and began to disperse from the area in all directions. Within minutes of hearing the gunshots, Gotfried Falkenstein, the superintendent of the Erie Gas Company, arrived.

Through the smoke, he saw the motionless body of Blackie Collins surrounded by a pool of blood, coal dust and puddles of tobacco juice.

Falkenstein phoned the police, who, in turn, notified Erie County coroner Dan Hanley. At headquarters, Chief Wagner assigned Detective Sergeants Richard Crotty and Lambertine Pinney to the case. All available patrolmen were ordered to descend on the Erie Gas Company with urgency.

After arriving at the scene, Wagner, Crotty and Pinney canvassed the immediate area yet failed to find the gunman or the revolver. They did, however, locate two transients. After being questioned by Chief Wagner, the two men admitted to witnessing the shooting, claiming the man responsible was a transient known as Erie Slim.

Wagner ordered both men to be placed under arrest as material witnesses and taken to headquarters, where they were presented with an array of mug shots of local criminals. The transients fingered a man named Edward Acheson as the shooter.

When Coroner Hanley arrived on the second floor of the retort house, he found Blackie Collins lying on his back on the floor, midway between a coal pile and a bench, his head nestled near an empty nail keg. A powder burn over Collins's left breast still smoldered, confirming Collins was shot at close range.

Hanley conjectured the shot resulted in instantaneous death and ordered the body to be removed to his undertaking rooms for an autopsy.

After Edward "Erie Slim" Acheson was identified as the shooter of Blackie Collins, Detective Sergeant John "Jack" Welsh and Patrolman William Brown set off for 352 West Twenty-Fourth Street, the home Acheson shared with his elderly mother. A flurry of telephone messages and telegrams were dispatched to various trolley stations and railroad junctions in the neighboring cities of Conneaut, Ashtabula, Dunkirk, Buffalo and Cleveland in the event the Acheson attempted to make a break for it.

That evening, as a frosty darkness consumed the city, patrolmen and detectives stretched out into the neighborhoods in search of Acheson. Detective Sergeants Crotty and Pinney led unsuccessful searches of innumerable saloons, railyards and fish houses along the waterfront and

then proceeded to search the Lake Shore
Railroad yards.

Meet Me at the Gas House

David Papineau, the superintendent
of police for the Lake Shore Railroad
in Cleveland, Ohio, received one of the
telegrams from Erie with great absorption,
as he was cultivated with Acheson's criminal
past. Acheson was suspected of committing
many crimes against the Lake Shore
Railroad, and he was the prime suspect
in the attempted murder of a signal tower
operator in Conneaut, Ohio, years prior.

Both men encountered each other in the
summer of 1907, after Papineau warned
Acheson to stay away from Lake Shore
property. Acheson, in response, threatened
to blow Papineau's head off.

As for Papineau, he informed Acheson
that he would be glad to return the compliment.

Staring at the telegram that evening, Papineau reminisced about his
meeting with Acheson years ago, believing the criminal would make good on
his threats should the opportunity present itself. Papineau resigned himself
to the real possibility that soon, both men would again cross paths.

Only this time, Papineau believed, there would be a bloodbath.

That evening in Erie, police officers arriving at headquarters for the
night shift were presented with a photograph and complete description
of Acheson.

As police launched a dragnet for Acheson, Coroner Hanley searched the
body of Blackie Collins in his undertaking parlor. The search of Collins's
clothing revealed a pipe, tobacco and three new rings tucked away in a
tobacco box. Two of the rings were plain bands, and the third was a seal
ring set with imitation opals, suggesting to Hanley the jewelry was of a
cheap variety.

Collins was "unusually good looking" for a tramp. His hair was black, his
features regular and clean, and he was dressed in trousers made of a striped
material, a blue shirt, a black coat and vest, a black overcoat and a black
slouch hat, all said to be in fair condition.

The bullet that ended Blackie Collins's life passed through all articles of
clothing and penetrated his heart, rendering death instantaneously.

"Blackie" Collins and Retort Room at the Gas House in Which He Was Murdered.

In the sketch of a section of the interior of the retort house is shown the bench upon which Collins sat, and the exact spot where the murder was committed is shown by the cross.

Opposite: A cartoon sketched by *Erie Daily Times* artist Walter Kiedaisch following the murder of Joseph "Blackie" Collins. *From the* Erie Daily Times.

Above: A sketch of Joseph "Blackie" Collins and the interior of the retort house where Collins was killed. *From the* Erie Daily Times.

As for Collins's identity, Hanley was unable to locate markings on Collins's clothes or possessions, but he later learned from Chief Wagner that one of the transients at headquarters informed him Collins formerly resided on Kingston Street in Lawrence, Massachusetts, and was related to a famous football player from Andover College who also met a tragic death.

Hanley forthwith sent a telegraph to Lawrence, Massachusetts, requesting further information from authorities there.

Detective Sergeant Welsh and Patrolman Brown's search of Acheson's lodgings at 352 West Twenty-Fourth Street proved futile, as Acheson was last seen around 4:00 p.m. and remained in the home only a few minutes before leaving. Believing Acheson came home to retrieve his revolver, they searched adjacent yards and streets bordering the Erie Cemetery.

These searches failed to locate Acheson. In the meantime, officers kept the home of Acheson's mother under constant surveillance throughout the night.

On the morning of February 28, Coroner Hanley received a telegram from Dan Collins of South Lawrence. The telegram read: "How was Collins killed? When? What is his first name?"

As Hanley prepared a response with a description of the murdered man, Chief Wagner received a call from the chief of police in Lawrence through the long-distance telephone, confirming the victim's identity as twenty-eight-year-old Joseph P. Collins, who was from a middle-class family in Lawrence, Massachusetts.

Wagner was later instructed that Joseph's brother Dan Collins was en route to Erie to take charge of his brother's remains and return them to Massachusetts for burial.

That morning, the front pages of the *Erie Daily Times*, the *Erie Dispatch* and the *Erie Evening Herald* recited the sensational details of the murder of Joseph "Blackie" Collins as police continued their manhunt. The *Erie Evening Herald*, optimistic that Edward Acheson would soon find his way behind bars at the Erie County Jail, wrote: "The fact that he is so well known to the police of various cities makes it very improbable that he can long escape arrest."

The desire for justice to be served was short-lived, as the case took a darker, cataclysmic turn.

A Soft Voice in the Night

Edward Gershon Acheson was born on June 23, 1871, to John and Anna Acheson (née Pendergast). The youngest of three children, Acheson grew up in Erie until the 1890s, when he left the city following the death of his father. Records are sporadic about Acheson's whereabouts until 1894, when he was sentenced to serve two years at the state penitentiary in Columbus, Ohio, after breaking into a railroad station in Olmstead Falls, Ohio.

After his release from prison, Acheson disappeared until 1900, when, in Michigan, he cracked a safe in Olivette and committed a burglary in Lapeer, using the aliases John Pruce and Ed Killian. Acheson was soon apprehended and sentenced to seven years of imprisonment at the Michigan State Penitentiary.

Edward Acheson's reputation made him a well-known criminal to authorities in cities such as Cleveland and Buffalo, where his mug shot and fingerprints were compiled with those of other infamous criminals of the Great Lakes region, earning him the moniker "Erie Slim."

Acheson was released from prison, only to be arrested again and charged with suspicion in June 1907 in Cleveland, Ohio. After his release in July, Acheson returned to Erie and was immediately placed under surveillance by Chief Wagner, who was well aware of Acheson's criminal history. After

The mug shot of Edward Gershon Acheson. *From the* Erie Daily Times.

some time, however, Wagner ceased surveillance when it appeared Acheson was attempting to live a decent, law-abiding life.

After purchasing a dray that summer, Edward Acheson attempted to engage in the draying business in Erie but was unsuccessful and later found himself unemployed by the winter of 1907. In November 1907, Acheson was arrested on a charge of suspicion in Cleveland and again released.

There was also the recent blowing of a post office in the nearby town of Edinboro, similar to others in neighboring New York, and Acheson was considered the prime suspect. The safes of these banks, small in size, were associated with the American Bankers' Association and under the protection of the Pinkerton Detective Agency.

Acheson's role in these attacks on local banks was not entirely clear, and his guilt appeared to rely on circumstantial evidence. Within time, an operative from the Pinkerton Detective Agency kept Acheson under surveillance. This, too, eventually ceased after no tangible leads were obtained.

Around 4:30 a.m. on February 29, 1908, Emma E. Hay, the superintendent of the Erie Cemetery, was awakened by a thumping sound against one of the windows of her home, located at the Chestnut Street entrance to the Erie cemetery.

Hay soon heard the faint sound of a man's voice.

Frightened, Hay awakened her assistant, Rita Eaton, who approached a window on the south side of the second floor. Straining to see through the morning darkness, she saw a man standing on the lawn below.

Eaton lifted the window and was greeted with a burst of cold air.

"Do you know who this is?" the man asked.

"Yes," Eaton shook her head. "It's Ed Acheson, isn't it?"

"Yes, it's me. I want to know how my mother is."

Eaton looked at Hayes with a perturbed look in her eyes. Both women knew Acheson's family and were aware of the crime he committed.

"She's in a terrible condition," Eaton replied. "She's just eating her heart out with worry over you."

"It's too bad," Acheson said, his voice soft yet distressed. "I'm awful sorry about the trouble I've caused her. Tell her for me that I did not mean to shoot that man, but I had to do it. He'd been following me around for a year or more, and I couldn't help doing what I did. I guess now that I've about reached the end, and I guess I will kill myself."

"Oh, you musn't do that!" Eaton cried out. "You wouldn't do that, would you?"

Despite the inescapable fear that paralyzed both women, Rita Eaton sympathized with Acheson, whose words appeared to be genuine and full of remorse.

"Yes," Acheson said, dropping his shoulders, "That's the only thing left for me to do."

"I'll call the police. I won't let you kill yourself," Eaton instructed in a stern manner.

"No, don't do that," Acheson responded. "You'd only make matters worse, you know, for then somebody else might go with me."

Feeling helpless, Rita Eaton was at a loss for words.

"You'd better go away. You might be caught here."

"No, not yet. I've got some more questions I want to ask you." Acheson pleaded, "How is my sister?"

"She's on her way home now."

"Who's with Mother?" Acheson said, his voice breaking.

"Mrs. Austin is with her."

"Then she will be well looked after. I'm glad of that." Acheson replied glumly, looking to the ground.

The former residence of Erie Cemetery superintendent Emma Hay. *Author's collection.*

"You'd better go away now," Eaton warned, preparing to close the window.

Acheson remained silent, as if contemplating what to say next as Rita Eaton looked on. A faint wind blustered through the bare limbs of the trees nearby as the snow continued to fall.

"Just have them follow my foot tracks in the snow, and they'll find my dead body at the end of them. Don't forget my message to my mother. Goodbye."

Rita Eaton watched as Acheson turned and walked away in a southerly direction, his feet crunching against the snow as he passed from sight among the tombstones.

What followed Acheson's absence was the eerie stillness of that dark February morning.

Eaton slammed the window shut and turned to Mrs. Hay. The two women discussed calling the police but feared Acheson was still watching them.

Eventually, they decided to contact Reverend Hugh L. Hodge, the pastor of Central Presbyterian Church. Emma Hay urgently phoned Reverend Hodge and repeated her concerns about Acheson. Hodge downplayed their fears, telling them he did not believe Acheson would bring further harm to anyone, let alone against either of them.

Reverend Hodge informed the women he would visit the cemetery that morning.

As morning came, the city radiated under a blazing sun and clear skies. Reverend Hodge appeared at Superintendent Hay's home around 9:00 a.m. and spoke with both women about the conversation that ensued hours before with Acheson. Outside, Hodge observed Acheson's footprints in the snow, which were "plainly discernible."

As Hodge ventured outside into the nipping air, Acheson's threats to take his own life echoed in Hodge's mind. Without further delay, he was determined to follow the footsteps, not sure of what he would discover.

A Tragic End to a Sordid Life of Crime

Following the footprints of Edward Acheson, Reverend Hodge discovered they led to the cemetery chapel.

As he inched toward the silhouette of the chapel in the distance, he made a ghastly discovery near the front steps.

Before him was Edward Acheson, sitting upright underneath the front porch, his head slackened to the side, with blood and brains scattered all about. A revolver was deposited nearby on the concrete porch, and near Acheson's feet was a quart-sized bottle half filled with whiskey.

Hodge bolted back to Superintendent Hay's home and notified the women that Acheson had died by suicide. Telephoning police headquarters, Hodge spoke to Chief Wagner before notifying Coroner Hanley of the discovery.

Chief Wagner and Detective Sergeant Pinney left for city hall and boarded a streetcar en route to the cemetery. As both men entered the cemetery, they cautiously approached the chapel, where they noticed Acheson on the front steps, apparently undisturbed.

Wagner and Pinney were soon joined by other patrolmen and a captain.

Turning to the captain, Wagner told him Acheson had reportedly died by suicide but ordered him to proceed with extreme caution. As the officers advanced on the chapel with guns drawn, it became clear that Acheson was deceased. Coroner Hanley arrived minutes later with an undertaker's wagon outside the chapel.

Hanley inspected the body, noting an entrance wound behind Acheson's right ear. The bullet had traveled clean through his head and exited through the left side of his skull. A pool of blood and brain matter next to Acheson's body was nearly frozen.

Chief Wagner ordered officers to search for the missing bullet; however, it was never located. For Chief Wagner, it was clear Acheson had prepared his end with a swig of whiskey before pressing the muzzle of the revolver behind his right ear and pulling the trigger.

At the request of Acheson's mother, Coroner Hanley removed the remains to the Burton and Sons Funeral Home so the body could be prepared for burial. Because of the circumstances, it was determined that no inquest into his death was necessary.

Wagner took charge of the blue steel revolver. The *Erie Evening Herald* described the fatal weapon in detail:

> *The gun was a Colt and of .38 calibre, instead of .32, as heretofore stated. It had six chambers, three of which were filled with loaded shell and unquestionably it was the bullet from this shell which put an end to the bloody career of "Erie Slim." Two other chambers were without shells and in the opinion of Chief Wagner these chambers held the two shells which Acheson fired at the gas house on Thursday afternoon, one of them cutting short the existence of "Blackie" Collins.*

Erie Cemetery Chapel. *Author's collection.*

Inspecting the revolver, Chief Wagner believed that after Acheson killed Collins, he removed the two empty shells, leaving four in the chamber, which he was prepared to use. A search of Acheson's body bore no additional cartridges in any of his pockets.

In one of Acheson's coat pockets, police found twenty-five dollars in currency, several pieces of paper and a pocketbook in which Acheson had scribbled a sentence bearing no date or signature: "I did not mean to shoot that man."

After visiting the chapel, Chief Wagner questioned Emma Hay and Rita Eaton about their discussion with Acheson. Arousing Wagner's curiosity were Acheson's claim that Collins had "been after him." This led Wagner to believe both men had been acquainted for some time and alluded to the possibility both committed criminal acts together, although Wagner lacked any definitive proof of this.

Wagner believed Acheson's fear of Collins would forever remain a mystery—taken with him to his grave.

The *Erie Evening Herald* wrote that Erie Slim had "lived a hard, sordid life of crime, he died much as he had lived, hunted by the police, a marked man;

A close-up of the front steps where Edward Acheson's body was found leaning against the railing on the left. *Author's collection.*

a man to be shunned by all of his fellow-men; a man with the life blood of another on his head and with a short shrift staring him in the face in the event of his capture."

Acheson's mother and sister were nearly paralyzed with grief when told of his suicide. It was noted by the *Erie Daily Times* that it was strictly ordered no admittance would be granted to the Acheson home until he was committed to the earth.

That afternoon, Daniel Collins arrived at Union Station and was taken to view his brother's remains at Hanley's Undertaking Parlor. Collins's appearance surprised many, including a reporter from the *Erie Dispatch*, who described him briefly: "D.F. Collins is a polished gentleman and it is difficult to imagine him the relative of a tramp. He has prospered in the express business and told Mr. Hanley to spare no expense in preparing his brother's body for burial."

Collins brushed off the nagging reporters, telling them he preferred not to talk much of his brother's current affairs, instead choosing to reflect on his brother's life, saying he was a young man of excellent prospects until a few years before, when he began to drink in excess and began associating with characters of bad company.

Daniel Collins told reporters from the *Erie Dispatch* that his brother worked as an express manager for the American Express Company in Lawrence, Massachusetts, until 1906. For nearly two years, the family had not heard of his whereabouts until the telegram was received from Coroner Hanley informing them of his death.

Joseph Collins was survived by both of his parents and three brothers, and because of her ill health, his mother had not been informed of his tragic death. After Daniel left Hanley's Undertaking parlor, he met with Chief Wagner at city hall, where he learned his brother's murderer had died by suicide, sparing the Collins family from a trial.

Around eleven o'clock that night, the casket containing the body of Joseph Collins was loaded from a platform at Union Station onto a train, where it began its final journey home to Lawrence, Massachusetts.

The plain black casket bore a silver plate that simply read: "At Rest."

On the afternoon of March 1, 1908, Chief Papineau of the Lake Shore Railroad arrived at city hall, accompanied by two detectives. In speaking with Chief Wagner, Papineau relayed information he received that indicated Acheson was in the process of leaving Erie for Albany, New York, to begin a series of criminal operations in that area. "So, that's the gun he was going to blow my head off with, eh?" Papineau marveled when handling Acheson's revolver.

It was a remarkable end for a criminal whose actions, according to Papineau, had cost the Lake Shore Railroad over $20,000 during his criminal career.

On March 2, 1908, the body of Edward Acheson was delivered to his mother's home. At almost exactly the same time, in a tragic coincidence, the body of Joseph P. Collins was received at the Collins family home in Lawrence, Massachusetts, where his family gathered in grief and prayer. The bodies of both men were forever intertwined in death as much as they were in life.

Presiding over the casket of her dead son, a dismayed Anna Acheson was comforted by her two daughters. Reporters and those who knew the family well predicted she would never recover from her son's death by suicide.

On March 3, 1908, the remains of Joseph Collins were interred at St. Mary's Cemetery in Lawrence, Massachusetts; 550 miles away, at the Erie Cemetery, Edward Gershon Acheson's body was lowered into the earth and also laid to rest just several hundred yards north of where he died by suicide. Perhaps as a measure of chagrin, his grave was left unmarked and remains so to this day.

The unmarked grave of Edward Acheson. *Author's collection.*

Although many condemned Acheson and his criminal past, one individual struck a different tone when writing an editorial for the *Erie Daily Times* on March 12, 1908. "Those who knew him best knew him only as a big-hearted, tender and helpful man, son and brother, for he was his poor mother's nurse, help and comfort all winter," the writer, whose moniker was simply "A True Friend," remarked. "For the last eight years he had certainly tried to live an honest life.…We hope and pray that the dear Lord will have mercy, and that at the last he heard and answered the prayers of the poor fellow as well as the lifelong and faithful prayers of the dear mother and sisters."

Following the murder of "Blackie" Collins in the retort house of the Erie Gas Company, Paul Mueller, the superintendent of the Erie Gas Company, barred all transients from the property, much to the disappointment of its employees who sought to appeal to the better nature of helping those in need.

From that moment on, all doors, both entrances and exits, on the property were locked.

Police were never able to determine Edward Acheson's whereabouts between 5:30 p.m. on February 27 to 4:30 a.m. on February 29, despite a thorough search of his known haunts, including local saloons and properties connected to Erie's criminal underworld.

The small bungalow home at 352 West Twenty-Fourth Street, where Edward Acheson's widowed mother grieved over the casket bearing her son's remains, still stands. Built in 1862, it remains one of the oldest homes in the upper west side of the city of Erie.

Anna Acheson passed away in 1914 at the age of eighty-one from diabetes and was buried alongside her son in the Erie Cemetery.

The history of the Erie Gas Company goes back as far as 1856, when the city installed gas lamps at the cost of twenty-seven dollars each. But they were installed in only a portion of the city, as a petition was presented from property owners, who were then taxed for the service. For many years, these lamps were not lit during the week and were ultimately phased out when electric lights started to appear in Erie in 1898.

By 1913, the City of Erie sought to save taxpaying citizens money by lighting its streets with electricity instead of natural gas. The Erie Gas Company criticized the move after the city discussed making a contract with the Erie County Electric Company, which was owned by wealthy businessman and philanthropist Charles H. Strong. The gas company warned that such a move could put it out of business. Mayor William J. Stern, whose recommendation was supported by local engineers, advised against the move, believing it was necessary for Erie to retain a gas manufacturing plant, even though it would be slightly more expensive.

Stern's recommendations were ignored, and the city council passed a resolution awarding a contract to the Erie County Electric Company. Because he had no legal authority, Stern was forced to sign the contract into law.

Despite promises that taxpayers would save money, the plan backfired. Instead of the city using incandescent lights, according to the original bid, incandescent lights were installed in only the center of each block where a gas lamp had been previously.

When the city paid the Erie County Electric Company all expenditures for the purchase of the arc lights, it led to both the Erie County Electric Company and Edison Company receiving record revenues. The Erie Gas Company managed to linger for some time until a $1,500 tax was placed on numerous gas mains that were not used throughout the city. This was the final nail in the coffin that ended Erie's only manufacturing gas company and the only company that could provide gas to citizens in a state of emergency.

By 1917, the remaining gas mains throughout the city were rendered useless due to leaks and required extensive repairs. This was evident even in

The former location of the retort house for the Erie Gas Company. *Author's collection.*

August 1915, when all of the gas and electric arc lights were cut off by the disastrous Mill Creek Flood. By then, it was too late, and soon, the Erie Gas Company went out of business. Gradually, the buildings at the foot of Sassafras Street fell into disrepair and became crumbling eyesores on the bayfront.

The large brick retort house where Joseph "Blackie" Collins met his untimely end was demolished by the late 1940s. The grounds where the retort house once stood are now virtually unrecognizable, and the property is now used to house boats that belong to members of the Presque Isle Yacht Club, leaving no trace of the tragic events that unfolded on that brittle February afternoon in 1908.

2

TRAGEDY AT MOORHEADVILLE

The Murder of George Cook and the Insanity of Ferdinand Fischer

*G*unshots splintered the pristine stillness of a beautiful, crisp autumn morning on September 10, 1908, in the neighborhood of East Fourth and German Streets. Soon, neighbors observed forty-seven-year-old Ferdinand Fischer of 413 German Street acting strangely, which was not out of the ordinary.

There was a reason he was nicknamed "Crazy Fischer."

It was only when Fischer, who was waving around a revolver, greeted neighbors that he told them if Max Conrad, whose property adjoined his home, set foot on his property, he would be shot. Fischer paced swiftly as he rambled on with a large corncob pipe hanging from the corner of his mouth. Fischer was determined to kill Conrad, and his actions created enough of a stir that soon, the City of Erie Police Department was bombarded with phone calls.

Detective Sergeant John "Jack" Welsh responded and set off for Fischer's home. A native of Waterford, Ireland, Welsh worked for the Erie Dispatch before joining the City of Erie Police Department as a patrolman. As a detective sergeant, Welsh was one of the more respected and experienced members of the police department.

Welsh arrived at 413 German Street to find Ferdinand Fischer in a state described as "raving mad." The aroma of gunpowder greeted Detective Sergeant Welsh as he stepped inside the home, and his attention was immediately attracted toward what appeared to be numerous bullet holes in the walls caused by a revolver. When questioned, Fischer mentioned

413 German Street, sketched by *Erie Daily Times* artist Walter Kiedaisch. *From the* Erie Daily Times.

nothing about having problems with his neighbors and instead told Welsh a "story of imaginary wrongs" caused by his brother-in-law George Cook. "That man Cook has come between me and my wife, and I'll kill him!" Fischer screamed.

Detective Sergeant Welsh remained calm as Fischer babbled, providing "a string of vile oaths" and "other wild statements." Familiar with Fischer's impetuous personality, Detective Sergeant Welsh managed to calm Fischer down before confiscating his revolver, which was fully loaded.

Welsh left Fischer's residence around noon and returned to headquarters, where he reported the incident to his superiors. It was later decided that the police would keep Fischer under surveillance out of an abundance of caution.

Before police returned to 413 German Street, Ferdinand Fischer left his home and purchased another revolver. He then went to Central Park in downtown Erie, where he patiently waited for the westbound trolley to North East. After departing sometime around 1:00 p.m., Fischer then instructed the conductor to let him off at the stop at Moorheadville.

When the trolley arrived at Moorheadville, Fischer stepped off and was greeted by his wife, Melda, and sister-in-law Emma Cook as they awaited the arrival of the westbound trolley to Erie so Melda could arrange for an upcoming medical operation. "Don't take that car," Fischer warned his wife and sister-in-law. "You will want to remain here today."

When the westbound trolley arrived, Melda Fischer briefly hesitated before climbing the trolley steps. Fischer's warning was disregarded by his wife and sister-in-law as they continued their trip into Erie, unaware of the tragedy that would occur.

As the trolley pulled away, both women watched as Fischer walked rapidly down Moorehouse Road toward the farm of George Cook.

Within minutes, Fischer turned off Moorheadville Road and sauntered down the dirt path leading to the Cook

Ferdinand Fischer as sketched by *Erie Daily Times* artist Walter Kiedaisch. *From the* Erie Daily Times.

farm. After crossing the wooden bridge that traversed Twelve-Mile Creek, he crossed paths with Hattie Kling, a neighbor of the Cook family.

Kling was surprised to see Fischer as he approached the nearby vineyard. "Well, Mr. Fischer," she called out, "I thought you had remained away from your family about as long as you could."

Fischer stopped and, "with a strange wildness in his eyes," glared toward King. "I have no wife and children," Fischer replied in an almost mechanical tone. "My home has been ruined by that man Cook, and I am going to kill him."

Without saying another word, Fischer continued walking in a brisk pace toward the vineyards on the Cook farm. Sixty-nine-year-old George Cook was plucking grapes from the vines with his mute son, Fred Cook, in the next row over. Farther down the field was Fischer's son, Thomas Fischer. "Look me in the face, George," Fischer demanded, stopping several feet behind Cook.

Cook, bent over with his back to Fischer, stood up and turned around after recognizing Fischer's voice. The faint smile on his face disappeared when he realized he was looking down the muzzle of a .32-caliber revolver that was less than three feet away.

Instantly, Fischer pulled the trigger, letting out a terrifying reverberation through the fields and woods. The first bullet passed through Cook's chest, just above his heart. A second bullet struck Cook in the jugular vein on the left side of his neck. As Cook crumpled to the earth, a third and final bullet embedded itself in Cook's left thigh.

Fischer loomed over Cook's body. Without saying another word, he turned and rapidly walked away, muttering to himself.

George Cook holding his grandson Harold King. *From the* Erie Daily Times.

Fred Cook, who fled the vineyard when Fischer fired off the first shot, burst into the kitchen of the Cook farmhouse, desperately gesturing to Hattie Kling and her nephew Arthur Johnson, who was working on the opposite side of the nearby creek. Grunting incoherently, Fred Cook imitated Ferdinand Fischer shooting his father, and after charging into the sitting room, returned with a photograph of Fischer, thumping his fingers against the glass with alarm.

Hattie Kling and Arthur Johnson looked out a nearby window and observed Fischer traveling over the last of the two wooden bridges before disappearing out of sight in the direction of the old Moorheadville schoolhouse.

King telephoned the City of Erie Police Department, informing Chief Wagner of the shooting. Within a few minutes, Chief Wagner and a group of officers secured an automobile and sped to Moorheadville. The Pennsylvania State Police were also on their way to Moorheadville, armed to the teeth with Winchesters as they traversed the countryside.

Coroner Dan Hanley boarded the westbound trolley for North East, accompanied by several newspaper reporters, around 4:00 p.m. Also on board the trolley was Walter Kiedaisch, a local cartoonist and artist for the *Erie Daily Times*.

As she waited for the coroner and police to arrive, Hattie Kling walked out to the vineyard and approached George Cook's lifeless body. After convincing herself that he was deceased, she draped a sheet over his body.

A reporter for the *Erie Daily Times* described the landscape of the George Cook farm, supplemented the day after the murder with a map drawn by the artist Walter Kiedaisch:

> *The road to the Cook farm winds down into the deep gully, where the school house stands. There the road branches off to the right and down into the bed of the creek. Two rustic bridges fifty feet apart are crossed and upon a slight elevation of ground a little distance beyond stands the Cook farmhouse. The road from the school house is a private one leading only to the Cook farm.*

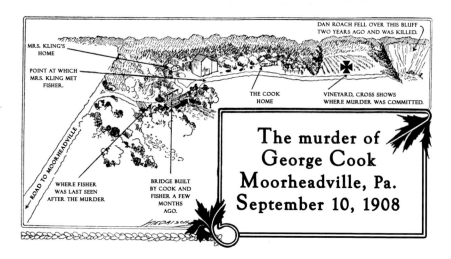

A map of the George Cook farm from the *Erie Daily Times* artist Walter Kiedaisch, enhanced by Gary Dombrowski.

> *From the house a path runs back a little ways through the vineyard and by the young orchard on the left.... The deep ravine through which Twelve-mile creek flows is a picturesque spot at this point. On the north and east of the Cook farm, almost perpendicular banks break the view of the lake.*

Following Coroner Hanley's arrival, a stretcher was crudely constructed, and George Cook's remains were removed to the farmhouse, where a careful examination was performed, establishing George Cook's death was instantaneous. In time, farmers in the vicinity gathered at the farm, and Hanley quickly impaneled a coroner's jury, securing testimony from Hattie Kling, Arthur Johnson, Thomas Fischer and several others.

The jury returned the following verdict:

> *We, the coroner's jury impannelled* [sic] *to inquire into the cause of the death of George Cook, of Harborcreek township, find, from the evidence offered, that the said George Cook came to his death on the afternoon of Sept. 10, 1908 sometime between the hours of 2 and 3 o'clock in his vineyard, in said township, by being shot three times from a revolver in the hands of one Ferdinand Fischer, of Erie, Erie county, Pa., with murderous intent.*

After the coroner's inquest, there was nothing further that could be done, and Coroner Hanley left Moorheadville for Erie on the 7:00 p.m. trolley.

Erie County coroner Dan Hanley. *From the* Erie Daily Times.

As the sun sank below the horizon, groups of men armed with guns and torches scoured the streams, woodlots and fields for signs of Ferdinand Fischer.

Beyond Mooreheadville, groups of country folk gathered with intense excitement on street corners while others gossiped in the seclusion of their front porches and parlors.

State police continued to search the countryside for Fischer, armed with Winchester rifles, ready to give battle. However, as darkness devoured the land, some believed Fischer had killed himself. Others spent the night arming themselves and locking their doors.

The legend of Ferdinand Fischer was born.

FERVID, INVECTIVE AND VILE ABUSE

Ferdinand John Fischer was born on December 20, 1861, to John and Catherine Fischer (née Diefenbach) in Hamilton, Ohio. Fischer's father, John, immigrated to the United States and settled in Erie, Pennsylvania, with his wife, Catherine, in the 1850s. After several of Ferdinand's siblings were born in Erie, the family later relocated to Hamilton, Ohio, in 1859.

Ferdinand's father, John, enlisted with the Second Ohio Heavy Artillery in September 1863 during the American Civil War and later attained the rank of lieutenant. For his actions during the war, he was awarded a commission and the rank of captain. By the 1870s, the Fischer family had moved back to Erie, where Ferdinand's father worked as a saloon keeper and was well respected within the city.

In 1880, Ferdinand Fischer was employed as a teamster in Erie, residing with his parents and siblings at their home located at 1012 State Street, and later married Minerva L. Alexander, a servant, sometime prior to 1883. Fischer's first marriage is believed to have produced somewhere around five children; however, records from this period are both inconsistent and uncorroborated.

Ferdinand Fischer's criminal history, at its earliest, can be traced back to the night of October 29, 1890, when the Eureka Iron Works was set ablaze. Fischer, spotted in the vicinity of the raging inferno, was arrested on suspicion of arson. Following his arrest, Erie Fire Department captain George Schweitzer of Hose No. 6 charged Fischer with the arson of the Eureka Iron Works.

Fischer was brought before Alderman Christian Swalley on the afternoon of November 8, 1890. The first witness called, William O'Lone, testified to seeing Ferdinand Fischer in the First Ward a short time after the alarm was given for the fire at the Iron Works. Another witness, Michael Dougherty, saw Fischer after he was placed under arrest by Erie City Police officer Thomas Culhane and confirmed Fischer's clothes were wet, as it had been raining all night.

Officer Culhane testified that he asked Fischer what he was doing in the area at the time the arson occurred. Fischer refused to answer Culhane's questions, telling the officer he would tell him some other time. Jacob Dudenhoefer, a captain with the City of Erie Police Department present at headquarters when Fischer was hauled in by Culhane, testified to Fischer's statements that were obtained after he was questioned.

After the commonwealth rested, Attorney George Ambrose Allen asked for the charges to be dismissed. District Attorney A. Elverton Sisson responded to Allen's request and claimed that although Fischer's actions on the night of the Eureka Iron Works fire were suspicious, he could not proceed with such minimal evidence and consented to Fischer's discharge.

In September 1891, a complaint was lodged against Fischer for assault and battery, yet these charges, too, were later dismissed. In October 1892, when Erie experienced fresh cases of diphtheria, Fischer, then employed by the city, was in charge of hauling lime to be distributed in the vicinity of the dump piles and other locations where poor sanitary conditions were reported.

Fischer's problems with the law resurfaced on September 15, 1894, when a local woman, Nettie Conway, alleged that while she was holding her ten-month-old child on the northwest corner of North Park Row and State Street, Fischer approached her and offered shelter from the pouring rain under his umbrella. Conway relented, and Fischer offered to carry her child. He then persuaded her to accompany him to the shelter of a nearby hallway.

As Fischer clutched Nettie Conway's child, he proceeded to make indecent advances toward her and used considerable force to try to detain her. Conway broke free from his grasp and started to run before she retraced her steps to grab her child. He made another attempt to subdue her but released his grip when the altercation attracted a group of pedestrians nearby who approached Fischer.

Fischer disappeared but was later arrested and charged with assault after Conway appeared at the police station and provided a description of her attacker, leading officers to suspect Fischer was responsible. At a hearing before Alderman Jacob Swap, it was later determined the evidence presented did not show intent on Fischer's part, and he was released with the charge dismissed.

It's around this time that Fischer disappears from the records in Erie.

America, meanwhile, was in turmoil when the USS *Maine* exploded in Havana Harbor on February 15, 1898, contributing to what is known as the Spanish-American War, which saw over seventy thousand Americans involved in the conflict.

Ferdinand Fischer appeared in Buffalo, New York, on June 16, 1898, when he enlisted with Company G of the Sixty-Fifth New York Infantry Regiment. Fischer's brief stint in the military would garner him only the rank of private, and on November 19, 1898, he was discharged.

By 1900, Ferdinand Fischer's marriage with Minerva had deteriorated, and the two were divorced. In June 1900, Fischer applied for what would

A present-day view of the George Cook property. The vineyard where Cook was murdered is visible to the left. *Author's collection.*

be his second marriage, and on June 4, 1900, he married Melda Armstrong of Erie. Several days after the wedding, Melda gave birth to a set of twins, a boy and a girl.

By 1902, Fischer owned a secondhand store on State Street between Third and Fourth Streets and appeared in an article from the *Erie Daily Times* in September 1902. The article stated he filed a charge of larceny against Dennis Crimmins for stealing an open-faced silver watch valued at twenty dollars from his store.

Fischer was arrested again in February 1905 and charged with stealing twenty-seven dollars from the office of J.L. Reid, a diamond contract businessman on North Park Row. Fischer, who entered the office to pay an assessment, stole money from the drawer and was arrested by Constable Arthur Dunn. As in previous cases, these charges were later dismissed.

By 1907, Fischer's mental faculties had already begun steadily deteriorating, and he had become known for his odd behavior and strange quirks. If any members of the general public found Fischer to be a danger, it was never outwardly reported; however, there was evidence Fischer's mental deterioration was not taken seriously by some.

One such instance occurred in 1907, when a political meeting was held at the Democratic headquarters in the Third Ward, in Dench's garage, as mentioned in an article from the *Erie Daily Times*: "Ferdinand Fischer took the platform and wanted to give expression to his political views, but was gently [and] firmly placed to one side. This incident occasioned much laughter."

Ferdinand Fischer was a ticking time bomb.

And it was only a matter of time before he exploded.

CRAZY FISCHER

A native of England, Cook immigrated to America in 1853 and settled in Erie County, where he lived for the rest of his life. Already the father of several children and a grandfather, on April 22, 1908, Cook married forty-year-old Emma Armstrong, the sister of Ferdinand Fischer's wife, Melda. At the time of his death, Cook had been married to his third wife for just under five months.

The relationship between Ferdinand Fischer and George Cook was remembered as being cordial. The two men were often seen working in Cook's fields and vineyards, and Fischer had recently helped construct the wooden bridges on Cook's property that spanned Twelve-Mile Creek. Fischer's relationship with his brother-in-law was so strong, it was said he had recently purchased adjoining property to be closer to the family and was intent on moving out of Erie altogether.

Those who knew Cook and Fischer struggled to make sense of the murder, and on the morning of September 11, 1908, another large posse under the direction of Pennsylvania State Police, assisted by County Detective Frank H. Watson, departed from North East and thoroughly searched the countryside until they reached Erie.

The search, like those before, turned up nothing pointing to Fischer's whereabouts.

That morning a substantial number of reports and telephone calls flooded the offices of the *Erie Daily Times*, the *Erie Dispatch* and the *Erie Evening Herald*. Some claimed Ferdinand Fischer's body had been found on the sandy beaches below the soldiers' and sailors' home, a victim of suicide. Others claimed he had been spotted in the city, which hastily sent a cadre of police officers and detectives traipsing throughout the city in search of the fugitive.

Those searches, too, came up empty-handed.

The *Erie Daily Times* seized on Fischer's mental state and notoriety in that morning's editorial:

> *There are several other incidents already brought to light, any one of which shows plainly enough the disturbed condition of Fischer's mind, and it is too bad that those close to him did not long ago take the necessary steps, unpleasant though they might have been, to protect him as well as others from the tragedy which occurred at Moorheadville yesterday afternoon.*

The *Erie Daily Times* also leveled blame against the City of Erie Police Department: "The best excuse the local police department has to offer for that sort of procedure appears lame in the eyes of the public, who maintain a police department for protection and not for the condoling of lunatics."

Throughout the rest of the day, the police department remained on alert, hoping Fischer would return to his home on German Street. All surrounding law enforcement agencies had also been sent telegrams about the crime and Ferdinand Fischer's description by the Erie County District Attorney's Office.

Yet no trace of Ferdinand Fischer appeared.

On September 12, 1908, hundreds of George Cook's friends and acquaintances congregated at the Cook farm in Mooreheadville for his funeral, where his body was laid out in the "sorrow-stricken" farmhouse. Reporters witnessed Cook's neighbors and fellow farmers act as pallbearers. There was also the fitting sermon from Reverend Dowds, the pastor of the Presbyterian church in Harborcreek, in which George Cook's life was celebrated.

Following the services, the funeral procession journeyed east to the outskirts of North East, where George Cook's remains were laid to rest in the Cook family plot in North East Cemetery.

At about the same time George Cook's remains were being committed to the earth, Ferdinand Fischer appeared at the home of his brother William Fischer near Six-Mile Creek. A well-respected Erie pharmacist, William Fischer was aware

The grave site of George Cook. *Author's collection.*

of his brother's crime and knew the police were searching for him. The brothers talked, with Ferdinand speaking in an unconcerned manner, asking how George Cook was.

At no time did Ferdinand Fischer hint that he knew Cook was in fact dead, his brother William later remembered. Knowing his brother had a propensity for violence, William managed to convince Ferdinand to hand over his revolver, which was in his pocket, and concocted a plan in which he informed his brother that the Erie County sheriff Henry Cogswell was searching for him to act as a guard in the Erie County Jail for the week.

Pleased with the opportunity, Ferdinand Fischer readily agreed and set out with his brother for Erie in his automobile.

When William and Ferdinand Fischer reached Erie, they stopped in front of the Erie County Jail in an attempt to locate Sheriff Cogswell but were unsuccessful. William Fischer parked his automobile at the corner of West Sixth and Peach Streets and ordered his brother to remain in the car while he sought out the sheriff.

While Ferdinand remained in the automobile, unaware of what was transpiring, William slipped out to the City of Erie Police Department, where he spoke with Detective Sergeants Lambertine Pinney and Richard Crotty and told both men that his brother was across the street in his automobile and that he needed assistance getting him into the county jail. Pinney and Crotty sprang into action and arrived at William Fischer's automobile.

Crotty opened the door and sat in the front seat while Pinney slid into the back seat next to Ferdinand Fischer. After carefully running his hands over Fischer's pockets, Pinney confirmed Fischer was not armed and then nodded to Crotty.

Arriving again at the Erie County Jail, Ferdinand Fischer was escorted inside by his brother and both detectives. Throughout the ordeal, Ferdinand Fischer spoke casually with the men, completely oblivious to the fact that he had murdered George Cook.

Ferdinand Fischer pleasantly told his brother he was looking forward to working for the sheriff. With "clever conversation," Ferdinand was led into his cell, his only objection being that he would not be able to wake in time to be ready for work if placed in a cell.

William Fischer promised his brother he would call the following morning, and soon, Ferdinand Fischer dozed off into a deep sleep on a cot in his cell. The brief respite from Ferdinand Fischer's bizarre behavior was short-lived, and soon, he angrily accused ex-warden Frank Moses of "exacting a toll of 25 cents per head from people who desired to come into the jail and have a look at him."

The Erie County Jail. Note the Erie County Courthouse in the background. *From the Erie County Historical Society.*

George Cook's nephew Albert King appeared before Alderman Jacob Swap on the afternoon of September 15, charging Ferdinand Fischer with willful and premeditated murder.

Prior to the preliminary hearing, which was scheduled for the evening of September 17, Dr. Morris S. Guth, superintendent of the State Hospital for the Insane in Warren, examined Ferdinand Fischer in his cell at the Erie County Jail at the request of Fischer's family to determine his mental state. Guth spoke quietly with Fischer for several minutes before informing him he was accused of murdering George Cook.

"Is it possible I have killed my best friend?" Fischer screamed, his voice convulsing with pain.

Fischer broke down, weeping bitterly as he wrung his hands in despair. He asked Dr. Guth why he had not been informed of the charges before, appearing to have been unaware of the prior appearances since his incarceration.

A reporter for the *Erie Dispatch* recalled: "His collapse was heartrending and it was several minutes before he could be calmed."

When removed to the corridor of the jail, Fischer was met by Sheriff Cogswell, who read aloud the charges against him. Fischer again broke down sobbing before mumbling incoherently about being ready to pay the penalty for his act and a speedy trial. He then rubbed his head roughly, complaining of soreness.

When returned to his cell, Fischer managed to regain his composure.

That evening, Fischer's preliminary hearing was held before Alderman Swap in the warden's office of the Erie County Jail in order to avoid a sensational crowd that had begun to spread outside. Fischer was represented by local attorney Charles A. Mertens, with District Attorney W. Pitt Gifford examining witnesses on behalf of the commonwealth.

When Fischer entered the warden's office, he took his seat without acknowledging the presence of anyone else, raising his hand to the side of his head, his eyes affixed to the floor.

A reporter from the *Erie Daily Times* witnessed Fischer's eccentric behavior: "Even while the details of his crime were being recited by the witnesses he gave no indication that he was aware of what was going on about him, the defendant remaining stolid and apathetic throughout, having no word to say nor even a look to give the witnesses or any of those present."

Testimony was obtained from Detective Sergeant Welsh, Hattie Kling, Arthur Johnson and Coroner Dan Hanley. Following the preliminary hearing, Fischer was committed without bail and returned to the county jail, with those present believing the trial would be held the upcoming Saturday before a grand jury.

On Saturday, September 19, 1908, Ferdinand Fischer was indicted by the grand jury in the murder of George Cook, with preparations made to prepare for a quick trial.

Since the preliminary hearing, however, Fischer had been examined by Drs. Wallace R. Hunter and J.E. McCuaig, who concluded Fischer was of unsound mind and believed "the disease from which he is suffering is such that he ought to be committed to some hospital for the insane where he can receive proper care and treatment."

On the afternoon of September 25, through Attorney Mertens, William Fischer presented a petition before Erie County judge Emory Walling, which requested Ferdinand be removed to the state asylum in Danville, Pennsylvania, until his upcoming trial. Walling reviewed the petition and later granted Fischer's removal to the state asylum, with Fischer scheduled to begin his journey to Danville that evening.

When it was time for Fischer to leave for Danville, he responded willingly and appeared cheerful as he kissed his wife, sister and other relatives who had gathered at the county jail. Fischer left, according to reporters, in "an apparently contented and self-satisfied state."

Not Guilty on Grounds of Insanity

After his brief hospitalization at the state asylum in Danville, Ferdinand Fischer returned to Erie on the evening of November 11, 1908, assisted by Police Chief Edward Wagner and his brother William for his upcoming trial.

Reporters from the *Erie Daily Times* who saw Fischer inside his cell at the county jail wrote about his return to Erie:

> *Fischer is looking the picture of health and appears as rational as he was ever in his life, and seems anxious to have his trial proceeded with. His stay at Danville, to which institution he was removed after being indicted, from all appearances, has agreed with him in every respect, but he does not evidence the concern which a rational man must feel in his situation.*

Ferdinand Fischer on Trial For Murder

Charles A. Mertens F. Vincent Gifford   William Fischer   Ferdinand Fischer
—Courtroom Sketch by Kiedaisch, of The Times Staff.

A scene inside the courtroom showing Ferdinand Fischer, his brother and the defense attorneys. *Sketched by* Erie Daily Times *artist Walter Kiedaisch; from the* Erie Daily Times.

The trial against Ferdinand Fischer opened on the morning of November 16, 1908, at the Erie County Courthouse, with local attorneys P. Vincent Gifford and Charles A. Mertens acting in Fischer's defense. District Attorney Gifford would prosecute the case for the commonwealth.

Fischer was led into the courtroom by Sheriff Cogswell and Deputy Charles Klemm and "mechanically" took his seat next to his defense attorneys and his brother William Fischer. Soon, Fischer stepped briskly forward with his attorneys and listened to the charges as they were read from the indictment by Clerk Gus Miller.

When asked how he wished to plead, Fischer hesitated briefly before murmuring, "Not guilty."

The drawing of the jury took roughly an hour, in which only thirty of the sixty men empaneled were called after Fischer was arraigned. Fischer remained bent slightly forward, his eyes downcast, showing excessive mental strain. His face, covered in stubble, appeared flushed. Behind Fischer sat his wife, Melda; his sister-in-law Emma Cook; and Constable Klemm, who had been deputized to guard Fischer. Sheriff Cogswell also shadowed Fischer nearby in case he grew violent.

District Attorney Gifford outlined the case for the prosecution, which lasted less than ten minutes, detailing the events of September 10, 1908, in dramatic fashion. Gifford promised the commonwealth would show the murder of George Cook had been committed not by an insane man but one of sound reason and discretion.

The first witness called to testify was Detective Sergeant John Welsh. Welsh testified to the events leading up to his entry to Fischer's home around noon on September 10. Welsh said when he attempted to look around Fischer's house, he was stopped by Fischer and reminded that he could not do so without a warrant.

Welsh testified that a search of Fischer's overcoat revealed a fully loaded revolver and shells, which he later confiscated. Fischer, Welsh claimed, accused his wife of being intimate with George Cook and told him Cook would "get his own dinner." Welsh testified Fischer had also telephoned the police station and again charged his wife with adultery.

On cross-examination, Welsh admitted to knowing Fischer for several years and acknowledged he had heard him referred to as "Crazy Fisher."

Emma Cook, George Cook's widow, testified to the encounter she and her sister had with Fischer when they waited to board the trolley car to Erie, adding that Fischer had a strange look in his eyes. She was not cross-examined, and the following witness, Mrs. Hattie Kling, testified to meeting Fischer on the dirt road leading to Cook's property just before the murder took place.

Kling testified Fisher's wife had been on the Cook property for roughly four days and, on the day of the murder, was returning to Erie. Kling recounted Fischer threatening to kill Cook and later heard three shots before her nephew Arthur Johnson ran to her home. The two of them then locked themselves inside for protection.

Johnson testified he was in the vineyard with Fischer's son Thomas around 1:15 p.m. Johnson confirmed that he witnessed only the first shot and saw Cook fall onto his face before he ran away. Ten minutes later, Johnson said, he returned to the vineyard along with Hattie Kling and found Cook deceased. The only mark that he noticed on George Cook's body was reportedly a small wound on his neck.

Under cross-examination, Arthur Johnson said Ferdinand Fischer's face was "dark red" when he pulled out his revolver.

Alfred Kling, the son-in-law of George Cook, spoke of the relationship between Cook and Fischer, claiming the two had always been close with each other and appeared to have been on the best of terms.

Coroner Dan Hanley testified how he was summoned to the scene of the murder and examined Cook's body. Fischer's attorneys attempted to object to Hanley's opinion on Cook's cause of death, claiming such a decision should be left up to the jury. When cross-examined, Hanley said he knew Fischer for many years, describing his disposition as "peculiar."

After the commonwealth rested, defense attorney P. Vincent Gifford opened and approached the jury. Gifford said softly, carefully, measuring his words:

> *Gentlemen, we are now trying a most peculiar case. It is not like the ordinary murder trial. In this case a man took the life of his closest friend, without an apparent motive. We will show that at the time of the shooting, for we do not deny the shooting, that he was not mentally capable of planning a murder, and from his various actions through life, many of which we will show you, we will endeavor to prove that he was not of sound mind at the time of the shooting, and has not been since. We will also show you that he has been in a hospital for the insane since September last. After having proved all of these things, we will ask you to return a verdict of not guilty, by reason of insanity.*

Local attorney Clark Olds was the first witness called by the defense. He testified to one occasion when Fischer came to his home, criticizing the actions of an appropriation for an extension of the public dock while at the same time suggesting Mill Creek be dredged so boats could traverse its waters, using the banks for purchases and deliveries. Olds testified he thought Fischer was insane and his ideas impossible without an extensive amount of funds.

Olds testified through cross-examination that he did not believe Fischer was of sound mind.

As the defense's expert witness, Dr. Guth testified to how he informed Fischer of George Cook's murder on the day of his preliminary hearing, and he remarked it was the first time Fischer realized he was responsible for the murder.

Fischer, Dr. Guth added, was unable to understand how he had been implicated in the crime. "In my opinion," Dr. Guth added, "his memory was a blank from a time before the shooting until I told him of it in the county jail on September 15."

"How long before the shooting would you say he had been in this condition?"

"That is hard to tell," Guth said. "I think his actions at the time were almost purely mechanical. He undoubtedly thought someone had injured him, and while revolving this over in his mind, he came to the conclusion that he should take the life of his brother-in-law. A sort of an insane fancy, which he immediately carried into action."

Guth added that while Fischer appeared to have improved since his return from Danville, his mental condition remained unchanged, despite Fischer telling Guth numerous details about his life, including when he was stationed in the Philippines during the Spanish-American War.

Under cross-examination, Dr. Guth was asked if he felt Fischer was mentally responsible for the murder. "In my opinion, he was not mentally responsible at the time of the shooting and has never been since."

Fischer, Guth continued, was liable to impulsive actions, which may have been due to his longtime usage of alcohol. Dr. Guth testified that individuals with this condition often make wild threats that result in them committing violent deeds. They ultimately have no moral perception at the time of the deed or afterward, similar to the pattern of Fischer's actions.

Because Fischer was not mentally capable of forming any motive at the time of the shooting, Guth said he felt Fischer's disease had progressed to the extent that it would only deteriorate with age.

"Would you recommend his being at liberty?" District Attorney Gifford asked.

"I would not," Dr. Guth responded. "He is a dangerous man."

When asked what kind of insanity he felt Fischer possessed, Dr. Guth responded without hesitation that Fischer suffered from "chronic alcoholic mania." When interviewed by Guth, Fischer claimed people were against him and attempting to harm him. Fischer was unable to understand why he did not kill those who wished to injure him, Dr. Guth said.

Concluding his testimony, Dr. Guth felt Fischer's condition had gradually progressed over a period of many years, but on certain occasions, it was much worse.

William Fischer was called to the stand and asked about Ferdinand's early life and upbringing, claiming his brother's mental issues started around the age of twelve or thirteen when he fell from a barn and struck his head. Since that incident, William said, his brother was never the same. Other incidents included his brother removing all his clothes and running around the yard. He also said he had to constantly be monitored by family members.

There was also evidence, William Fischer suggested, of mania from a young age, as his brother had a tendency to start fires, often setting them close to the family's home and barn. When he was twenty years old, William

Fischer said, Ferdinand owned a team of horses that were malnourished after being fed sawdust and shavings. William said that his brother was unable to mentally comprehend why the horses were getting thin.

A brief history of the family revealed one of Ferdinand's uncles died in an insane asylum. There was also Ferdinand's involvement in reporting false fires and his suspected involvement in arson and other crimes in Erie, which usually resulted in his release due to a lack of evidence.

Asked about the events following the murder of George Cook, William Fischer testified he first saw his brother that Saturday following the shooting, when Ferdinand appeared at his home and entered his room acting strangely. William asked Ferdinand what was in his pocket, and his brother surrendered his revolver to him.

Ferdinand, William Fischer said, was completely unaware of his surroundings and had not realized he shot and killed George Cook. From there, William recited his plan to take Ferdinand to the Erie County Jail. William Fischer also agreed that he did not feel his brother understood he was responsible for George Cook's murder until he was informed of the matter by Dr. Guth.

The remaining witnesses that day provided medical testimony supporting the claims of Fischer's mental instabilities.

Drs. Charles B. Chidester, Frank Walsh and Friend L. Hall testified to treating Fischer for several years for syphilis, with Dr. Walsh acknowledging Fischer still suffered from the incurable disease. All three physicians believed Fischer was insane and that he had been so for a number of years. Dr. James Silliman, the last witness called that day, testified that while Fischer was not his patient, he knew Fischer well and did not believe he had been in his right mind for many years.

The following morning, November 17, Drs. H.H. Foringer and Charles A. O'Dea testified that they, too, treated Fischer for syphilis, which they felt had a significant effect on Fischer's mental health. Both doctors also added that they believed Fischer's syphilis contributed to fits of epilepsy.

Emma Cook, George Cook's widow, spoke about Fischer's insanity from past experiences, corroborating the testimony of others. She again testified to meeting Fischer when he arrived in Mooreheadville prior to the murder.

Melda Fisher believed her husband had shown signs of insanity since the beginning of their marriage, and she thought him crazy. Ferdinand, Melda Fischer added, would have fits that lasted for days while complaining of significant head pain. Two days prior to the murder, George Cook visited the Fischer home in Erie and stayed for supper. Melda Fischer testified that nothing out of ordinary occurred between the men, and her husband warmly bid him farewell before he departed.

That same night, Ferdinand suddenly became crazed and threatened to kill Melda while holding a knife. He also insisted men were in the house, individuals Melda Fischer knew to have been dead for several years. Out of fear for her own safety, she left the next morning to stay with her sister and brother-in-law in Mooreheadville.

Additional witnesses added to the volume of stories surrounding Fischer's insanity, with several doctors presenting evidence that Fischer suffered from an attack of epileptic insanity beginning on Labor Day, which continued for several days. Fischer, the doctors testified, was unable to recall events that occurred during this time.

This, coupled with the fact that Fischer took no steps to prevent detection or conceal his escape after George Cook's murder supported that he was insane when the murder was committed. Fischer's defense attorneys added this as they presented their closing arguments.

Judge Emory Walling charged the jury that in accordance with the law, the verdict they reach must be either "guilty of murder in the first degree" if it was decided that Fischer was sane and merely in a passion when he shot Cook or "not guilty on grounds of insanity."

Walling stressed that even if Fischer had temporarily recovered from his insanity, he was still subject to epileptic outbreaks, according to expert medical testimony, and that the epileptic or alcoholic insanity Fischer possessed made him a danger to the public. After forty minutes of speaking to the jury, just before 4:00 p.m., Judge Walling released them to begin their deliberations.

At 5:45 p.m., almost two hours later, a verdict was reached.

Spectators and reporters in the courtroom noticed the downcast expression of countenance on Fischer's face was replaced with an expression of being worry-free yet emotionless. Fischer refused to look at Judge Walling or members of the jury, keeping his head upright as the verdict was announced.

"Not guilty, by reason of insanity."

Following the verdict, Ferdinand Fischer was escorted back to his cell in the Erie County Jail. Later, his mood became significantly more communicable, cheerful and approachable. That evening, Fischer had reportedly "brightened up considerably," and he was allowed to visit with his wife and family, which he enjoyed every moment of, according to reporters.

On November 19, 1908, assisted by Sheriff Cogswell and his brother William, Ferdinand Fischer was transported to North Warren aboard the

The State Hospital for the Insane in Warren, Pennsylvania. *From the Pennsylvania State Archives.*

one o'clock train on the Pennsylvania Railroad. That afternoon, Fischer's wife, his children and his other family bid him goodbye at the county jail before his departure. Fischer admitted to looking forward to his journey to the hospital in Warren, as he was relieved that he did not have to return to Danville, which he had a great dislike and fear of.

When inmates arrived at the State Hospital for the Insane in Warren, Pennsylvania, they passed through a pair of iron gates before advancing down a long, narrow roadway, which led to a large, sandstone-colored Dickensian building that dominated the other buildings nestled in the hilly Pennsylvania countryside, complemented with a sprawling landscape of gardens and trees.

Construction on the state hospital in Warren, Pennsylvania's third mental institution, began in August 1873, and it began admitting patients in 1880. When Ferdinand Fischer arrived through the iron gates at the State Hospital for the Insane in Warren in November 1908, the beginning of his admittance record states: "Nov. 19—Ferdinand Fischer is committed to the hospital on an order of the Court of Quarter Sessions of Erie Co., Pa. A Case of Mania."

Hospital records for Fischer's admittance to Warren, while not extensively detailed, provide an insight into his mental deficiencies, which, as doctors expected, only continued to decline.

Some of the notes within Fischer's file provide the following details:

December 17, 1908: Neuritis is extending, both arms and one leg involved, most of it imaginary or feigned.
February 1, 1909: Complaining frequently about food, clothing, no privileges, etc.
March 1, 1909: Constantly causes trouble, at times sullen.

June 1, 1909: Is still troubled with his leg; requires watching and at times is a nuisance; complains constantly.

While at Warren, Fischer was often visited by friends and relatives. On several occasions, Fischer's delusions were so grand that he became persistent in telling guards and orderlies at the state hospital that soon, he would be return to his home in Erie.

On the night of June 20, 1909, Ferdinand Fischer made good on his promise. He escaped.

THE MANHUNT HAS STARTED

On the night of June 20, 1909, inmates of the Fifth Ward of the State Hospital for the Insane in Warren were escorted to the chapel for church services around 8:00 p.m., leaving Ferdinand Fischer and another inmate alone on the north side of the second floor of the hospital building.

As soon as Fischer confirmed they were alone, he approached the inmate, telling him he needed to walk up and down the corridor to enjoy the cool summer breeze that was fluttering in through one of the bay windows.

With the other prisoner obeying his commands, Fischer sprinted to the opposite end of the corridor, where he was out of sight and, with several saws he procured, began cutting at the bars on the window. After cutting through two of the bars, Fischer took grease and applied it to the remaining bars, pulling them apart. Then, taking two heavy blankets from his bed, Fischer tore them into strips and fastened them together to make an improvised rope.

Tying one end of the torn strips to the remaining bars, Fischer slipped through the window, wearing only a pair of slippers and a dark, striped shirt, rappelled down the side of the building and vanished into the darkness.

It was only after the other inmates and orderlies returned between 9:00 p.m. and 9:30 p.m. that Fischer's escape was discovered. An alarm was quickly sounded, and a posse composed of asylum attendants and employees congregated on the grounds of the hospital.

A pair of saws used by Fischer to facilitate his escape were later located under a fresh mound of earth near the north end of the building, which led hospital authorities to believe that a fellow patient working at the hospital provided them to Fischer.

Throughout the night, aided by the Warren Police Department, the posse hunted for Fischer in the nearby woodlots, streams and fields surrounding the hospital but were unable to locate him.

News of Fischer's escape did not reach Erie until around 10:00 a.m. on June 21, 1909.

Chief Edward Wagner notified all officers on duty to guard the railroads entering and leaving the city, especially those with freight trains, and every additional effort was made to monitor the dozens of roadways. Updated descriptions of Fischer's appearance, in which he possessed a mustache and well-trimmed hair, were forwarded to cities and towns in the tri-state area. Wagner also detailed officers to keep Ferdinand Fischer's home at 413 German Street under constant surveillance should he attempt to visit his wife and children.

By the afternoon, police had become almost inundated with reports of possible sightings of Fischer in the city. Harry Mehl of the Erie Trust Company told a reporter from the *Erie Daily Times* that he saw a man near East Fifth and German Streets whom he recognized as Fischer, but he said he was not able to get a clear enough look at him. Mehl, who was well acquainted with Fischer, only realized the significance of his sighting after William Fischer told him of his brother's escape.

Wild rumors deluged the offices of the *Erie Daily Times*, the *Erie Evening Herald* and the *Erie Dispatch*, sending reporters scurrying throughout Erie County.

In Warren, authorities questioned the prisoner who was left with Fischer on the night of his escape. Authorities suspected the possibility that Fischer's family members helped him escape, but this was later discounted as it was well known Ferdinand Fischer's family approved of his admittance to the hospital. Some of the inmates of the state hospital gossiped Fischer had used magic to escape. Others adamantly insisted a carriage was waiting for Fischer to escape and carried him away.

Despite having no clues about Fischer's current whereabouts, his defense attorney, P. Vincent Gifford, felt Fischer likely hopped aboard a freight train out of Warren and would be found in the woods several miles south of the city there, his capture possible within a few hours.

Additional reports trickled in from as far away as Meadville, suggesting a recent incident near Conneaut Lake could have involved Fischer. When two men in a boat arrived at the naphtha boat launch on Oakland Beach in Conneaut Lake, they were confronted by a man lying nude on the shore in the grass. As the men approached him, the nude man leapt to his feet and darted off into the woods.

This report was also corroborated by two other individuals who reported seeing a naked man on the public road who darted into the woods when spotted that morning.

Whether the sighting was ever conclusively confirmed as being Fischer has never been ascertained.

By Wednesday, June 22, 1909, authorities of the State Hospital for the Insane in Warren remained baffled, unsure of what next steps should be taken to track down Fischer with almost the entire county near the hospital having been thoroughly searched. Authorities no longer believed that Fischer was near Warren; instead, they believed he was hiding out somewhere near the outskirts of Erie.

A rigorous search of the neighborhood around Fischer's home and detailed searches of every freight train entering and leaving Erie revealed no additional clues.

The superintendent for the State Hospital for the Insane in Warren, Dr. Guth, was pessimistic when it came to Fischer's apprehension. "If Fischer keeps sober, he will probably never be apprehended," Dr. Guth told Volney B. St. John, a deputy warden of the Erie County Jail who was in Warren on business. "Liquor alone, in my estimation, will bring about his capture."

As days turned into weeks, the paranoia surrounding Ferdinand Fischer's escape gradually diminished. In August, Attorney Charles A. Mertens filed a petition in court asking to sell Fischer's property to meet the demands of creditors. The petition was later granted.

With the end of 1909 in sight, authorities were very much still searching for Fischer, this time led by Frank H. Watson, the shrewd yet colorful Erie County detective in the employ of the Erie County District Attorney's Office. Watson's investigation had flown under the radar of local reporters and the mildly curious as he tracked Fischer from Pennsylvania, into Ohio and finally as far as away Chicago, Illinois, where authorities eventually lost track of him.

The big break for Watson came in November, when he was informed that Ferdinand Fischer had written to his family, telling them he was employed as the head of a strike-breaking crew of switchmen in Minneapolis, Minnesota. The letters also gleefully mocked authorities who had pursued him all over the country.

Watson corresponded with authorities in Minnesota, who confirmed Fischer's presence in the city. Fischer, however, soon became aware he was being monitored and started adjusting his habits and daily life, such as working at irregular intervals.

In early January 1910, Detective Watson traveled to Minneapolis assisted by County Commissioner M.J. Smith of Corry, Pennsylvania, to search for Ferdinand Fischer. Fischer realized authorities traced him to Minneapolis, and on Thursday, January 6, he quit his job, demanding transportation back to Chicago, where he initially enlisted as a strike-breaker. The railroad agreed. On Saturday, January 9, 1910, Fischer planned on arriving at the St. Paul Freight House to collect his pay near the union depot and then depart the city.

For the first time, law enforcement was one step ahead of Fischer, and as soon as he approached the payment window of the St. Paul Freight House, he was swarmed by several police officers, who placed him under arrest. While searching Fischer's pockets, officers found a one-way ticket to Chicago and twenty dollars in currency.

Speaking to the officers, Fischer informed them their work would be useless because he would fight extradition to Pennsylvania. Later that night, while locked up at the local county jail in Minneapolis, Fischer was confident he would not be extradited, boasting, "I have engaged an attorney to look after my case and will show these guys a trick or two before I get through."

The following day, Fischer was arraigned before a judge in Minneapolis probate court on the warrant presented by County Detective Frank Watson, charging him with insanity.

Fischer took the stand with an air of confidence. As he looked around the courtroom, Fischer admitted to killing his brother-in-law with a story so convincing, it was reported to have convinced anyone. The court also assigned three physicians to examine Fischer and collected testimony from three members of Fischer's switching crew.

All the doctors agreed that Fischer was sane, and with the evidence presented, Probate Judge Smith ordered Fischer's release.

When Fischer was released, Detective Watson attempted to secure another warrant, this time charging him with being an escaped convict, but the county attorney for Hennepin County refused to issue it, telling Watson had he taken out a warrant on that charge initially instead of charging Fischer with insanity it was likely the state would have ordered Fischer's return to Pennsylvania on requisition papers.

Because of this, authorities in Pennsylvania were not able to legally arrest Fischer for extradition.

Later that afternoon, District Attorney Gifford received a telegraph from Detective Watson notifying him of Fischer's release following the preliminary hearing. As Detective Watson's additional appeals to the Minnesota attorney were later rebuffed, the blunder to arrest Fischer created an uproar in Erie. For one of the few times in his career, Detective Watson escaped the criticism of the general public.

The *Erie Daily Times* wrote:

> *Mr. Watson is not a lawyer and was placed at great disadvantage when he had pitted against him the skillful attorney that Fischer was shrewd enough to employ. But it does seem to a layman that the proper place for the determination of the fugitive's mental condition was in the courts of Pennsylvania. The action of the Minnesota court does not look like fair treatment of this state.*

County Detective Watson and County Commissioner Smith returned late on the night of January 12. Adding further salt to their wounds, Ferdinand Fischer decided to ride in the same railcar with both men as the train journeyed from Minneapolis to St. Paul, losing no opportunity to keep the passenger car in an uproar in clear view of Watson and Smith.

Before disembarking at St. Paul, Fischer bid both men farewell, telling them he preferred the climate in Minnesota to that of Pennsylvania.

In Erie, officials continued to express frustration that an attorney was not sent with Detective Watson and County Commissioner Smith to Minnesota, adding they knew nothing about plans to apprehend Fischer until Watson and Smith were already in Minneapolis. It was suggested the district attorney or county solicitor should have taken personal charge of the case, determining such a venture should have not been handled by a detective.

Several months later, in an odd change of events, on the afternoon of March 4, 1910, Ferdinand Fischer appeared before a police officer in Youngstown, Ohio, and surrendered. Notified of Fischer's surrender in Youngstown, County Detective Watson left Erie the following morning and arrived in Youngstown just before noon.

When questioned by Watson, Ferdinand Fischer said he intended to work in Youngstown and later invite his wife and children there, but those plans fell through. "I couldn't stand it any longer," Fischer insisted. "I had to give myself up, but I am not insane."

Both Watson and Fischer returned to Erie shortly around 2:00 p.m. that same day.

With news spreading in Erie about Fischer's capture, Watson anticipated a large crowd would greet them at Union Station. As the train crawled into the station, Watson led Fischer to the rear of the railroad car and hopped off at Sassafras Street. From there, both men boarded a streetcar and traveled to the Erie County Jail, where Fischer was temporarily placed in a cell to wait to be presented before a judge.

Two reporters from the *Erie Daily Times* found Fischer shaving his face and observed that he looked the same as he had at his original trial, only older. Fischer joyfully welcomed both men, shaking their hands. Providing a brief interview, Fischer admitted he admired the work of the *Times* and received it often under the alias of Joe Heintz in Cleveland, Ohio.

One of the reporters asked Fischer if he was crazy.

Fischer paused, pressing the straight razor against his neck. "Do I look crazy? Am I crazy?" asked Fischer, his eyes widening as he gestured.

Both reporters looked on in silence.

"I am crazy in this state," Fischer said shaking his head, mumbling to himself. "Mr. Watson is the only sane man. Whatever he says is the truth—I guess."

Not one to be lost on formalities, Fischer requested the *Times* change his address on file in Cleveland to that of the Erie County Jail. Before he could get settled in his cell in the presence of both reporters, two wardens appeared from Warren to transport him back to the state hospital there.

Questioned about his return to the State Hospital for the Insane in Warren, Fischer did not object, claiming it was merely a matter of business.

Several weeks later, on May 3, 1910, Ferdinand Fischer escaped again, this time in the company of another inmate, William Dunham, after successfully removing a set of bars from a window at the end of the corridor he was housed in.

It was hours before anyone noticed both men were missing.

A manhunt was launched throughout the Warren area and the surrounding hamlets and boroughs. County Detective Watson was notified of the escape, and again, local authorities were placed on alert. It was shortly before 9:00 p.m. when Dunham was captured and returned to Warren. Uncorroborated reports reached the *Erie Daily Times* in Erie that Fischer was apprehended near Frewsburg, New York, outside of Jamestown.

The reports proved correct, and around four o'clock on May 4, Fischer was recaptured after asking for food from a local farmer in Jamestown, New York. The farmer, after giving Fischer breakfast, noted a peculiarity about him after Fischer said he had traveled from an asylum in Warren. After Fischer departed the farm, the farmer reported the incident to authorities, who tracked Fischer to Jamestown, where they arrested him before he was able to board a train out of town.

Fischer was again returned to the State Hospital for the Insane in Warren, and again, he continued to cause trouble for the staff and inmates there, with the records stating the following actions:

> *September 1, 1910: Has been confined to room; is sullen and hard to get along with; goes out walking, to ball games, etc.*
> *March 1, 1911: Patient ordered Joe Wilson to stop signing and Wilson struck him; patient then struck back and dislocated one of his fingers; he bullies the other patients but gets along fairly well; refuses to speak to one of the assistances and never neglects an opportunity to tell the physician how many patients he has abused, etc.*
> *June 1, 1911: Condition remains unchanged; still bullies the other patients and makes himself disagreeable in numerous ways; is going outside regularly to the different amusements, etc; is somewhat more friendly but refuses to speak to the supervisor Mr. Healy; eats and sleeps well.*
> *June 15, 1911: Pushed Wm. Holder because he went into his room and he fell and cut a gash over his eye; patient claims he did not intend to hurt him.*

Within time, Fischer was granted the opportunity to roam the grounds of the state hospital freely. Those aware of Fischer's relaxed restrictions assumed it was only a matter of time until he escaped again when the opportunity presented itself.

Fischer's third and final escape occurred on the afternoon of August 12, 1911, when he was walking the grounds of the hospital and simply vanished.

He was never seen or heard from again.

HIDING IN PLAIN SIGHT

On May 24, 1948, Dr. Robert H. Israel, the superintendent of the Warren State Hospital, formerly the State Hospital for the Insane in Warren, wrote a letter to Erie County judge Elmer L. Evans. In his letter, Dr. Israel claimed Fischer's whereabouts had remained unknown since September 1912.

The letter continued:

> *Inasmuch as this patient had been committed on Further Order of Court, it is necessary for us to keep his name on our parole records as an escaped patient. It is our feeling that there is little use in continuing any patient in*

the status of an escaped patient for a period longer than ten years. If he
were still alive he would be 86 years of age. The probabilities are that he
is dead or is an inmate of some other institution....If the Court concurs
in this attitude, we would appreciate authorization to discharge this patient
from our hospital records.

On October 26, 1948, Judge Evans agreed and authorized the discharge of Ferdinand Fischer from the records of Warren State Hospital.

Both men were unaware, however, that Fischer was still very much alive.

For 112 years, Fischer's whereabouts have remained unknown. Although the years progressed without a mention of Fischer in the press, those who knew him feared his reemergence, with theories abounding about where he was or who else he could have possibly harmed.

As it turned out, the whereabouts of Ferdinand Fischer were in front of investigators all along, and the trail led right back to Fischer's family.

Following an unsuccessful attempt to petition for her husband's release, Melda Fischer moved to Rochester, New York, in 1912. By 1914, Ferdinand Fischer would reappear in Rochester, New York, and was later arrested by police after throwing a lighted lamp at Melda, breaking two of her fingers at their home at 15½ Lorenzo Street.

Fischer appeared in police court on October 14, 1914, and was paroled for a year for the offense.

The following year, Fischer and his family relocated to 41 Brayer Street in Rochester, along with four of Fischer's children, and the 1915 New York census lists Fischer's occupation as "engineer." Not long after the census recording, Ferdinand Fischer again disappears from public records. It was believed that Fischer's abuse against his wife and mental problems became too much for the family and, in turn, caused Fischer to again abandon them.

He would not appear again until 1925.

On December 23, 1925, Ferdinand Fischer was admitted to the National Military Home for Disabled Volunteer Soldiers in Dayton, Ohio. Now sixty-four, Fischer was described in their records as being five feet, ten inches tall, with a white complexion, blue eyes and graying hair. Fischer listed his occupation as "millwright" and a nearby cousin, George Diefenbach, as his closest relative.

Other records show Fischer filed a divorce petition in common pleas court in Dayton, Ohio, on February 15, 1926, which listed his wife's address in Rochester, New York. On July 8, 1926, Fischer's petition was granted. By then, his health continued its decline, as he suffered from hemiplegia, causing paralysis to the left side of his body. Sometime between 1927 and 1930, it is possible Fischer temporarily resided in Toledo, Ohio, before he then is shown in records of the National Military Home for Disabled Volunteer Soldiers in Jefferson City, Tennessee, where he would be discharged on May 27, 1930.

Fischer was still residing in Jefferson City, Tennessee, on November 6, 1931, when he married sixty-four-year-old Kittie Broyles of Greeneville, Tennessee. Broyles, the widowed daughter of a Baptist minister, was a member of the Freewill Baptist Church in Greeneville. While insurance companies and law enforcement agencies occasionally communicated about the disappearance of Ferdinand Fischer, he remained undisturbed with his third wife as they lived in plain view in Greeneville.

On November 2, 1948, at 9:15 p.m., Ferdinand Fischer died at the age of eighty-seven at his home at 101 Unaka Street in Greeneville, Tennessee, from myocardial failure due to hypertension.

It is unknown if Fischer's criminal past was ever known to his third wife and those in the Greeneville community. Fischer's body was removed to the Doughty-Stevens Funeral Home, where a funeral was held on the morning of November 8. His body was then taken to the Andrew Johnson National Cemetery, where he was interred with full military honors.

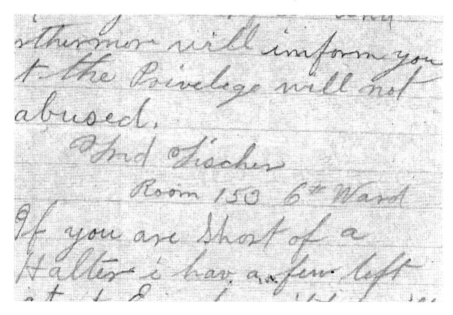

A close-up of a letter that was written by Ferdinand Fischer while he was an inmate at the State Hospital for the Insane in Warren. Note Fischer's peculiar signature. *From the Pennsylvania State Archives.*

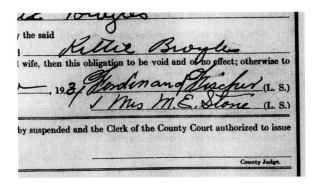

Ferdinand Fischer's signature on his marriage docket from 1931. *From the Pennsylvania State Archives.*

Following his arrest in 1914 in Rochester, New York, Fischer appears to have steered clear of involvement in criminal activities, although this is not entirely confirmed. It is possible that while on the run, he used the name John Ferdinand Fischer or John Fischer as an alias. Despite these possibilities, it was also possible that by the 1920s, Fischer's mental and physical health ailments prevented him from becoming involved in further crimes.

George Cook's widow, Emma, also relocated to Rochester, New York, where she lived with her sister until her death in 1929. Melda Fischer claimed her husband was deceased by 1920, according to census records and additional inquiries by law enforcement and insurance companies. This presented the impression that she knew nothing of her husband's whereabouts. She died from nephritis in 1931.

In April 1930, the Prudential Insurance Company opened an investigation into the disappearance of Ferdinand Fischer. A manager with Prudential, Fred Ohl, wrote to the superintendent of Warren State Hospital, H.W. Mitchell, indicating that there was an insurance policy of value on Fischer's life.

Mitchell responded to Ohl's inquiries, confirming Fischer had escaped in 1911, the year before he assumed the role of superintendent there, and referred Ohl to the law firm of O'Brien and McSweeney in Rochester, New York, claiming they possessed additional information. He told Ohl that the hospital, too, inquired about Fischer in 1929. "I know nothing of the man personally, except in that we should be pleased to locate him if possible," Mitchell wrote.

After his death in 1948, a letter was sent to Mabel Lindgren, one of Fischer's daughters. The letter, written by a male acquaintance of Fischer's, informed Lindgren of her father's death and also included details of his life before his passing. Whether any of Ferdinand Fischer's other children knew of his death is something that will forever remain a mystery. Perhaps they

A present-day view of the roadway leading away from the George Cook farm showing the route Fischer escaped on in 1908. *Author's collection.*

felt that by revealing Fischer was alive, it would only bring more attention than desired. Or perhaps they still believed they were better off without his presence, which had brought so much pain and heartache before.

As for George Cook's farm, it remains in Harborcreek, although the landscape has changed considerably since the murder in 1908. One can still walk along the vineyard where Ferdinand Fischer pumped three bullets into George Cook's body on that brisk September afternoon before disappearing into history.

As for Ferdinand Fischer, one of Erie's most infamous insane murderers, after his legend came to an end in 1948 in Tennessee, he remains buried there to this day.

3

"WE THIS BLACK HAND..."

The 1909 Extortion and Blackmail
of Charles Hamot Strong

The Black Hand—the name alone is enough to chill one to the bone, at least to those who lived long ago, when the words became synonymous with an infamous Italian extortion racket often associated with gangsters of the Camorra and Italian mafia.

By the 1900s, the Black Hand was established in the Italian communities of major cities across the country, including New York City, Chicago, Boston, Philadelphia and New Orleans. The group's tactics involved sending a letter that threatened to inflict bodily harm, kidnapping, arson or murder. Demanding a specified amount of money to be delivered to a predestined location, the letters were decorated with a variety of symbols, such as a smoking gun, noose or skull and bones. The most infamous of these symbols was a symbolic and crudely drawn black hand.

The fear and paranoia experienced by those targeted by the Black hand reverberated through Erie when local businessman and philanthropist Charles Hamot Strong received threatening letters attempting to extort money.

The case, one of the most infamous to occur in Erie's history, began on March 31, 1909.

Like a large, roaring beast, the four-story mansion of Charles Hamot Strong and his wife, Annie Wainwright Strong, towered over the corner of Peach and West Sixth Streets, perched on the edge of Millionaire's Row in downtown Erie, Pennsylvania. The majestic house, layered with beautiful blue sandstone and trimmed with rustic yellow Pompeian brick, stood out against the last remnants of snow that spotted the property and sidewalks.

The roofs of the mansion, elaborately trimmed with terra-cotta and slate, twinkled under a bright sky that afternoon as a letter arrived addressed to Strong. The envelope, small in size, was covered in red ink and had been postmarked earlier that day.

Slicing open the envelope with a penknife, Charles Strong unfolded the letter, which said the following:

> *Dear Sir—We this <u>Black</u>*
> *<u>Hand</u> demand $500 in $10*
> *bills. We demand you to put*
> *money under bridge on railroad*
> *tracks that goes to log cabin*
> *if you do not put the money*
> *there on April 3 at 8:30 P.M.*
> *sharp you will find that*
> *your home will be blown to*
> *bits. If you try to betray us*
> *you will be killed. Beware*
>
> *Signed*
> *The Black Hand*

Believing the letter to be the well-crafted prank of an educated man, Strong discarded the contents, paying them no mind. He and his wife were no strangers to letters of a threatening nature. In the days that followed, Strong continued about the city, often engaging in business as president of the Erie County Electric Company.

Charles Strong watched as April 3, 1909, came and went without incident.

All was quiet until April 5, when Strong received a second letter written in the same penmanship as the first letter. Strong carefully examined the contents of this letter:

> *Dear Sir—You fooled*
> *us once. But this*
> *is your last chance.*
> *We warn you to*
> *put money, $500 in $10 bills under*
> *bridge that leads*
> *to log cabin on tracks*

if not you will be
shot <u>dead</u> from ambush.

Beware   *Black Hand*
turn over

BEWARE
Be on bridge at
8:30 P.M. Monday
April 5, 1909 with money

REMEMBER

Concerned, Strong decided he would wait until after 8:30 p.m. on April 5 to decide what steps he would take. That evening, he phoned Chief Edward Wagner of the City of Erie Police Department, postal inspectors with the

The Strong Mansion. *From the Erie County Historical Society.*

Dear Sir— We this Black Hand demand $500 in $10 bills. We demand you to put money under bridge on railroad track that goes to log cabin if you do not put the money there on April 3,— at 8.30 P.M sharp. you will find that your house will be blown to bits. If you try to betray me, you will be killed. Beware

Signed

The Black Hand.

April 3, 1909

Dear Sir— You fooled us once. But this is your last chance. We warn you to put money under bridge that leads to log cabin on tracks if not you will be shot dead from ambush. Singled.

Beware Black Hand turn over.

BEWARE

Be on bridge at 8.30 P.M. Monday April 3, 1909 with money.

REMEMBER

Left: The first letter mailed to Charles Strong on March 31, 1909. *From the* Erie Dispatch.

Right: The second letter mailed to Charles Strong on April 5, 1909. *From the* Erie Dispatch.

The location of John Eberle's drugstore, 404 West Eighth Street, where the first letter was mailed to Charles Strong on March 31, 1909. *Author's collection.*

United States Postal Service and County Detective Frank H. Watson to report the contents of the letters.

The first letter was postmarked March 31, 1909, around 9:00 a.m., and mailed from John Eberle's Drugstore at 404 West Eighth Street. The second letter, postmarked April 5 around 11:30 a.m., was mailed from the corner of West Fourth and Cherry Streets.

Nothing peculiar was noted about the paper used in the letters, which dozens of stores in the city sold. There was also nothing to indicate that the Black Hand had been involved, apparent by the obvious lack of spelling errors and crude writing often seen in such letters.

By attempting to extort money from Strong, those responsible for the Black Hand letters had decided to take on one of Erie's wealthiest men, whose history was strongly connected to the beginning of Erie itself.

WRETCHES OF THE BLACKMAILING CHARACTER

Charles Hamot Strong was born on March 14, 1853, to Landaff Strong, a well-respected local physician, and Catherine Cecilia Hamot. Both of Charles's parents were descendants of Erie County's oldest and most prominent families. Martin Strong, Charles's grandfather, came to Erie County in 1795 and settled in Summit Township. His other grandfather, Pierre Simon Hamot, a French émigré, settled in the county in 1802.

After graduating from Yale University in 1877, Strong returned to Erie, where he practiced law under local attorney Frank Gunnison, who later became a judge in the Erie County Courts. Bored with the prospects of law, Strong became a bookkeeper and shipping clerk with the Mt. Hickory Iron Works, where he later became president.

After serving as president of Mt. Hickory Iron Works, Strong served as president of the Union Coal Company of Shamokin, vice-president of Youghiogheny River Coal Company of Illinois and president and director of the Erie and Pittsburgh Railroad.

On September 8, 1881, Charles Scott married Annie Wainwright Strong, the daughter of former congressman and Erie mayor William Lawrence Scott, in New York City. Their marriage produced a daughter, Matilda Thora Strong, in 1882.

Known in Erie as a man of great culture, Strong was respected as a local civic leader and noted philanthropist. His interests in physics and electricity

Charles Hamot Strong. *From the Erie County Historical Society.*

led him to become a pioneer in the electric light industry. After becoming acquainted with Thomas Edison, Strong became one of the leaders in developing the first streetlights for the city of Erie and, in 1886, organized Edison Electric Light and Power Company, later named the Erie Electric Company, where he served as president until his death.

Strong also used his influence in Erie for other means. In 1902, he purchased the Dispatch Publishing Company and oversaw the *Erie Dispatch* newspaper. His wife, Annie, owned the *Erie Evening Herald* newspaper. They often butted heads with rival newspaper, the *Erie Daily Times*, which referred to the Strong-owned newspapers as "the twins."

Charles Strong was visible to the public, often seen riding his bicycle or walking through downtown Erie, always well dressed in a tailored suit and hat. With his chiseled jaw, Hungarian-styled moustache and piercing eyes, Strong was easily distinguishable. "He looked like he would be a military man when he walked. He walked like a general," sixty-six-year-old Irene Ritter reminisced to the *Erie Morning News* in 1974. "Sometimes we would say, 'Here comes the general.'"

In 1911, local automobilist Jack Curtis paraded around the city in a large Simplex with four enormous cylinders and a Klaxon horn. When his motor stalled one morning at the corner of West Sixth and Peach Streets, backfiring with a tremendous explosion, it angered Annie Strong to the point that she had Curtis arrested and thrown into the city jail as a public nuisance.

Hearing about Curtis's arrest, Strong, an automobile enthusiast himself, came to Curtis's rescue and had him released. As Curtis was released from his jail cell in police headquarters, he was greeted by an apologetic Charles Strong. "Awfully sorry, old man," Strong apologetically said to Curtis. "You know how women are."

Charles and Annie Strong were also known to host within the walls of their mansion lavish parties, which included guests like former president William H. Taft. Parties and dinners were also hosted west of the city on Charles Strong's estate known as Somewhere.

The Somewhere Estate encompassed around one hundred aces, with fifty acres owned individually by Charles and Annie Strong, and it has belonged

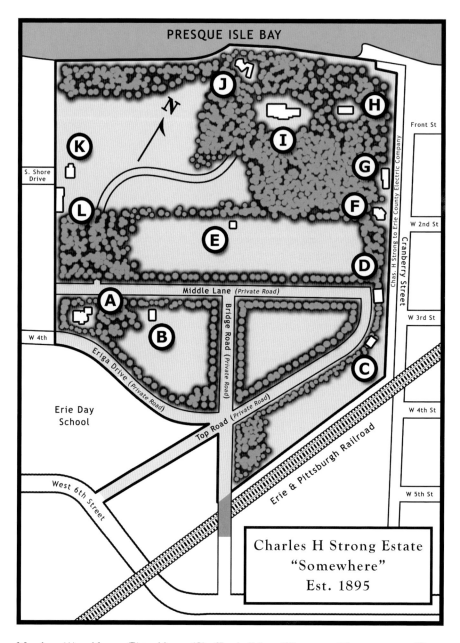

Map key: (A) residence; (B) tool barn; (C) office building; (D) cottage; (E) water tower; (F) lodge; (G) garage; (H) laundry; (I) the log cabin; (J) the "lookout"; (K) residence; (L) garage.

Looking west, Charles H. Strong and an unidentified man pose on the road leading to Strong's log cabin on the Somewhere Estate. *From the Erie County Historical Society*.

Another view, looking east, of Strong's cabin on the Somewhere Estate. *From the Erie County Historical Society*.

to the Hamot and Strong families since 1823. The estate was situated on a cliff overlooking Presque Isle Bay, dotted with woodlots, an apple orchard, bountiful gardens and buildings that housed caretakers and others under the Strongs' employ.

Irene Ritter, whose uncle Charles Storch later worked as a bodyguard for the Strongs, spent time at the Strong estate as a child, playing on portions of the property, including the surrounding garden, populated with hundreds of fruits, vegetables and currants nestled within its decorative brick walls. "If he [Strong] saw us on it, he'd wag his finger back and forth and we'd get down right away. He was very strict," Ritter remembered.

The property had dozens of private roads, pathways and walkways, with the roads lined by three-and-a-half-foot-tall walls constructed using rock and boulders. These fine stone fences were well maintained and looked after and also allowed access to the shore of Presque Isle Bay and a small pier.

One of the private roadways, decorated with the electric-powered streetlamps, snaked north through the property to Strong's log cabin, which was constructed using stone boulders and log-framed siding accentuated by the use of tree trunks, both interior and exterior. The cabin manifested the wealth and character of Strong's fortune.

Inside, the cabin was richly decorated and adorned with elegant fixtures, and it had a private wine cellar in the basement. The interior finish of the walls was done by the Constable Brothers Company, one of Erie's leading contracting firms during the period.

The living room and dining room sat under polished open-beamed ceilings, constructed using uncut tree trunks laid out in a lateral pattern. The A-shaped great center hall welcomed guests under a two-story-tall cathedral ceiling and a large stone fireplace which continued onto the second split-level floor, where an opposite fireplace opening faced Charles Strong's den and working area.

The dining room, decorated with a brick wood-burning fireplace, added charm to the cabin and was located off the kitchen. On the second floor were numerous bedrooms, complete with built-in bookshelves and hand-rubbed wall paneling of a natural wood motif.

South of the estate was a wooden bridge that spanned the Erie and Pittsburgh Railroad tracks. It was this bridge, mentioned in the Black Hand letters, where Charles Strong was ordered to leave $500.

After receiving the threatening letters, Charles Strong remained stoic to those around him, fearing only for the safety of his granddaughter Thora Scott-Ronalds. After notifying the authorities about the letters,

Strong increased security around his mansion and estate, hiring additional bodyguards to patrol the grounds for prowlers.

One of the bodyguards hired on April 8 was Charles Storch, who had faithfully served the family before.

At the Strong mansion, paranoia poisoned the halls, rooms and servants' quarters. Charles Strong refused to deviate from his normal schedule, and in the days that followed, he continued about his daily business, with the only significant event occurring one night when Charles Strong entertained friends for dinner at his cabin. One of Strong's employees spotted a man lurking among the woods on the grounds of the estate and approached him, asking him what his business was.

The prowler disappeared into the darkness.

On April 9, 1909, Charles Strong announced a reward for $1,000 for the capture of the blackmailers responsible for sending the threatening letters. Presenting facsimiles in the *Erie Dispatch* and the *Erie Evening Herald*, Strong remained steadfast in his attempt to bring those responsible to justice. "The above pleasant letters were written in red ink, not necessarily suggestive of blood, but presumably so. They were delivered through the United States mail." Strong pointed to the letters, "I will pay one thousand dollars for the arrest and conviction of the writer and sender of these letters."

The *Erie Daily Times* praised Strong's actions: "Mr. Strong is to be commended for the step he has taken and the sooner the community is rid of wretches of the blackmailing character the better."

Strong's reward created temptation among private detectives, who flooded Erie in the hopes of locating those responsible and securing the reward. One of those private detectives, sixty-seven-year-old Gilbert Boyd Perkins Sr., was hired by Charles Strong to hunt down the blackmailers.

Perkins, visiting Erie after his work in the kidnapping of Billy Whitla in Sharon, Pennsylvania, was a well-known and respected private detective who owned the Perkins Detective Agency in Pittsburgh, Pennsylvania.

Born in Venango County on September 7, 1842, Perkins was a veteran of the American Civil War, in which he served as a second lieutenant in Company C of the 150th Pennsylvania Volunteer Infantry and was wounded at the Battle of Gettysburg on July 1, 1863. Perkins later married Sarah Evaline Hall and lived in the Borough of Waterford before serving as a member of the United States Secret Service. After a distinguished and respected career with the secret service, Perkins created his detective agency in Pittsburgh.

As soon as he was hired, Perkins began his hunt for the letter writers.

Strong believed the matter would soon be solved, and on April 9, a third letter arrived at the Strong residence and was later discovered to have been mailed from the corner of West Fourth and Cascade Streets. Strong never revealed the contents of the third letter, only confirming it contained the same threatening braggadocio of previous letters.

Private Detective Gilbert B. Perkins Sr. *From the* Pittsburgh Press.

In the days that followed, those in Erie were captivated by the recent murder of sixty-nine-year-old Vinnie Young, who was found in her home on West Seventeenth Street with her head bashed in. The sensational headlines about the extortion letters created further scandal in the city.

Inside the Strong mansion, however, the paranoia reached its zenith on the night of April 11, 1909.

Around 8:20 p.m. that night, six Romanian immigrants ventured from the countryside to Erie in search of three of their fellow immigrants who had been arrested and charged with being drunk and disorderly. The Romanians wandered along West Sixth Street, unsure of where the police department was located. Soon, they stopped at a home and were provided directions leading them to a large brick building overlooking Central Park.

At 10:00 p.m., the Romanians, mistaking the Strong mansion for city hall, climbed the front steps and approached the front doors, where they attempted to enter. The jostling of the front doors, followed by sounds of fists thumping against the wood, alarmed one of the maids inside, who alerted Annie Strong.

Thinking the Romanians were the blackmailers making good on their promises to cause murder and mayhem, Annie Strong hurried to a telephone and called police headquarters. Detective Sergeant Jack Welsh answered the phone and spoke to a frantic Annie Strong.

Welsh sprinted to the patrolmen's room and armed himself with a revolver. "Get your guns and hurry to Strong's residence!" Welsh cried out. "The blackmailers are there!"

Inside the mansion, servants and maids cowered in fear as Annie Strong ran to a rear door to meet the officers as they charged inside. Other groups

The City of Erie Police Department in 1905. Police Chief Edward Wagner (*second from left*) sits next to Captain William F. Detzel. In the second row, clearly visible (*from left to right*), are Detective Sergeants Jack Welsh, Lambertine Pinney and Richard Crotty. *From the Erie County Historical Society.*

of patrolmen swarmed the mansion from all directions, armed to the teeth as they ordered the six men to surrender.

Detective Sergeant Welsh soon learned of the Romanians' mistake and found the men meant no ill will whatsoever to the Strongs or those inside the mansion.

For the servants and maids inside the mansion, the incident was a clear example of the effect the extortion letters had on not only the Strongs but also those who were employed by them. Some of the servants were so shaken up by the rumors that a bomb had been placed under the home that they feared staying there.

That night, following the false alarm at the mansion, police received a call from a man who claimed he knew the men responsible for writing the threatening letters. The man, identified as twenty-one-year-old Joe Enas, later arrived at the police station, where he spoke to Chief Wagner and was questioned further.

He gradually revealed more information: that there were three, possibly four, young men involved. He knew the boys personally, he told detectives, and believed he was present when one of the letters was mailed. Despite possibly knowing those involved, Enas denied knowing of the plot to threaten and extort Charles Strong.

The men were soon identified as seventeen-year-old Carl Penetzke, nineteen-old Earl Vincent McBride and eighteen-old John Costa. After the identifies of the men were confirmed, Chief Edward Wagner detailed Detective Sergeants Richard Crotty and Lambertine H. Pinney to arrest the men, assisted by Patrol Officer Anthony Williams.

Being Persons of Evil Minds and Dispositions

Detective Sergeants Crotty, Pinney and Patrolman Williams set off with a patrol wagon and driver to reach the home of Carl Penetzke. They arrived around 5:30 a.m. on the morning of April 12, 1909, at 902 West Third Street. Penetzke was awakened by the police, and the arrest warrant was read to him before he was removed from the home and placed into the wagon.

Searching through Penetzke's home, officers located a bottle of red ink, similar to the type used in the letters.

Police then entered the home of John Costa at 1056 West Sixth Street, where he was arrested. As Costa was led to the wagon, he asked detectives if they had arrested Penetzke. The detective sergeants confirmed they had. A bottle of red ink, similar to the one found in Penetzke's home, was found inside Costa's home.

Within a few minutes, Penetzke was joined by Costa inside the wagon. Police also located another bottle of red ink at Costa's residence. Police then arrived at the home of Earl McBride, located on the corner of West Fifth and Cascade Streets, where he was arrested and placed inside the wagon, which was now en route to the police station.

As the three men were arrested, Joseph Enas was informed by police he, too, was being arrested while detectives further investigated his role in the extortion plot.

Detectives were curious about why the young men would have engaged in such a crime. Carl Penetzke, whose family was well known in Erie, had no criminal record. Neither did John Costa or Joseph Enas. Earl McBride was the one who had a criminal record, his most recent crime having occurred in the fall of 1908, when he was with a man who was shot and killed by a constable while attempting to steal chickens.

Patrolman Anthony Williams and Detective Sergeants Richard Crotty and Lambertine Pinney were responsible for apprehending the blackmailers. *From the* Erie Daily Times.

That morning, rumors of the arrests leaked to the public and those in the city excitedly attempted to scarf up every detail in the arrests.

After being booked at the police department, each of the men was placed in a separate cell, and one by one, they were separately taken to the office of Chief Wagner, where they endured grueling interrogations. Several hours later, the men started to crack when Carl Penetzke confessed he was responsible for writing the letters. John Costa and Earl McBride also confessed they knew of the letters and were involved in the plot. The men admitted all three letters had been written at the Penetzke home.

Their reason for wanting to extort money from Charles Strong? They wanted to travel to Denver, Colorado, where "they could have enjoyed real western life."

Although the three men confessed their intent to extort money from Charles Strong, they vehemently denied any intention of harming him. Yet they felt confident Strong would eventually cave and pay the money as ordered.

Once the men confessed to their roles in the crime, a court stenographer was brought to the office of Mayor Michael Liebel Jr., and that afternoon, the men were again questioned by Chief Wagner and Private Detective Gilbert Perkins.

As Carl Penetzke, John Costa and Earl McBride awaited their arraignment, Annie Strong personally thanked each of the officers at her home for solving the case. Charles Strong, who was visiting city hall the day of the arrests, also congratulated each of the men.

After conferring with Mayor Liebel and Chief Wagner, Charles Strong was presented with the transcripts of the confessions from the men and extensive details of the case that assured him that the ordeal had been solved. Upon hearing this, Charles Strong allowed the details of the arrest to be released to the public.

Joseph Enas was soon released after police were confident he was in not involved in the extortion plot against Charles Strong, but for reasons unknown, he was rearrested the next morning.

Later that night, the three men were arraigned before Alderman John Scheer, and each pleaded guilty to the charges presented. In default of $5,000 bail, each were committed to the Erie County Jail, where they would await possible trial during the upcoming May term of quarter sessions court at the Erie County Courthouse.

While the men were in their cells, a reporter for the *Erie Daily Times* said Penetzke, Costa and McBride appeared to be "taking their arrest in a rather unruffled manner."

What came as a shock to those keeping up in the case was that the men arrested were not the cold-hearted criminals they envisioned were responsible. Speculation was rife among the local papers, as they believed Penetzke and Costa would receive light sentences, while McBride, due to his recent involvement with the courts, would be dealt the harshest sentence of the three.

Unable to post bail, Penetzke, Costa and McBride remained incarcerated, and throughout the halls of the Erie County Courthouse and within legal circles in the city, it was rumored further charges would be filed against them for illegal use of the United States Mail, which would see the case wind up in federal court. This would create further confusion if proven to be true, due to potential jurisdictional disputes between the county and federal governments.

On April 21, 1909, around 8:00 p.m., Carl Penetzke, John Costa and Earl McBride were brought before U.S. commissioner Harry L. Moore and held on $500 bail. The following day, the three defendants were present for a hearing, signaling the steps had been taken by federal authorities to bring criminal charges. George P. Craighead of the United States Postal Service provided information before the U.S. Court of the Western District of Pennsylvania in Erie.

Another hearing on April 22, held around 3:00 p.m. before Commissioner Moore, was conducted by Assistant U.S. district attorney N.S. Williams of Pittsburgh. The three men were ordered to be taken before federal court, under the charge of U.S. deputy marshal Robert H. Chinnock. As federal authorities pushed ahead with their plans to bring federal charges, U.S. district attorney Williams made arrangements with District Attorney Gifford for the men to be prepared for the trial in May.

Should the cases against the three young men be disposed of to the satisfaction of federal authorities, Williams believed their indictments would be presented through the federal court system around July. After the hearing, Williams informed the families of the men that they should secure the best lawyers they could afford so the case might be presented on its merits only.

On the afternoon of May 10, 1909, Carl Penetzke, John Costa and Earl McBride presented themselves before Judge Emory Walling and pleaded guilty to the charges of conspiracy to extort by sending threatening letters. District Attorney Gifford also announced that arrangements had been made with federal authorities to allow the county courts to have primary jurisdiction in the case, eliminating the possibility of federal charges being filed.

Judge Walling sentenced the men on May 25, instructing that for the first letter sent to Charles Strong, John Costa and Earl McBride would each be sentenced to three years in the western penitentiary, and for the second letter, Costa's sentence would be suspended, with McBride receiving an additional year to be served consecutively.

Especially harsh with McBride, Judge Walling said that if he had done as he believed he should have with McBride in November 1908, he would have sent McBride to a reform school. Walling reminded McBride that several highly respected citizens interceded on his behalf, and in going against his own judgment, Walling suspended that sentence.

Left: Judge Emory A. Walling. *From the Erie County Historical Society*.

Opposite: Carl Penetzke, later in life, working as a Linotype operator for the *Erie Daily Times*. *From the* Erie Daily Times.

McBride, Walling continued, owed the people of Erie County an apology. "When either a boy or man abuses an act of kindness, there is no further use for him to expect any favors at the hands of the court," Walling said.

When dealing with Carl Penetzke, Walling believed that he was the "best behaved" out of the three men, and for that reason, he ordered him to be committed to the Industrial Reform School at Huntingdon. Judge Walling told Penetzke that if his conduct warranted it, he could be released within a year.

Colonel J. Ross Thompson, a respected attorney, appeared in court on behalf of Charles H. Strong and Robert Chinnock and spoke on behalf of the prisoners before Judge Walling.

After sentencing, the men served their respective punishments. Since then, the extortion case of 1909 has been overshadowed and forgotten throughout history.

Carl Penetzke arrived at the Industrial Reformatory School in Huntingdon, Pennsylvania, as assigned inmate no. 6732 on May 26, 1909. Documents within Penetzke's court file indicate that due to his good behavior and rehabilitation, he was paroled from the Industrial Reformatory School on January 17, 1911.

From then on, he remained a law-abiding citizen, married and raised his children in Erie. By 1916, Penetzke was working as a Linotype operator for the *Erie Daily Times*, a position he held for over forty years before retiring and

later suffering a stroke in his west side home at the age of seventy in May 1962. Widely respected among those in Erie, Penetzke was posthumously honored by the Tri-State International Typographical Conference in 1962.

After his discharge from the Western Penitentiary, Earl McBride enlisted in the United States Army in 1914 and returned to Erie after his discharge in June 1919. In July 1925, while being chased by Prohibition agents, McBride wrecked a truck that was carrying over sixty cases of alcohol and was arrested and charged with possession and transportation of intoxicating beverages. After pleading guilty, McBride paid a $750 fine and was released.

McBride steered clear of the law afterward, and following the extinction of Prohibition, became employed as a long-distance truck driver. He later married and became a traveling salesman late into the 1930s. Earl McBride died in August 1938 from throat cancer at the Veterans Administration Hospital in the Bronx, New York.

John Costa also returned to Erie after his sentence in the Western State Penitentiary, married and started a family. When given money to purchase a chicken for a Christmas dinner in December 1918, Costa instead used the money to buy gin. Deciding not to face the ire of his wife, Costa broke into a chicken coop and was arrested and convicted of the crime. He served a sentence of one year and three months.

Costa continued to have run-ins with the law for the remainder of his life; these included charges of disorderly conduct, assault and battery and surety of the peace. He died at the age of fifty in January 1942.

Gilbert Perkins, outsmarted by the Erie City Police Department in pursuing the three blackmailers in 1909, returned to Pittsburgh and continued his work with the Perkins Detective Agency. On February 8, 1911, after the Scott Mausoleum in the Erie Cemetery was desecrated, the Perkins Detective Agency was assigned to the case, only to be discharged several days later after Charles and Annie Strong again received letters purporting to be from the Black Hand.

In a strange twist, Perkins was later arrested for sending the threatening letters to the Strongs, along with the manager of his detective agency in the city of Philadelphia, Charles Franklin, a disgraced former detective from Erie. Both Perkins and Franklin maintained their innocence but were later convicted and sentenced to prison terms at Fort Leavenworth Penitentiary.

Due to his declining health and good behavior, Gilbert Perkins was released from Fort Leavenworth and returned to Pittsburgh before he relocated with his family to the Borough of Waterford, Pennsylvania. Perkins stayed out of the public eye in the remaining years of his life as his family operated the Green Goose Inn in Waterford and died on February 9, 1926, at the age of eighty-three, maintaining his innocence in the 1911 extortion case against Charles and Annie Strong until the very end.

After the second extortion case, both Charles and Annie Strong sought to keep their private lives out of the press. In the years that followed, their marriage deteriorated, and by 1918, Charles Strong permanently resided in his log cabin on the Somewhere Estate, while Annie lived in the mansion.

Shortly after Charles Franklin and Gilbert Perkins were sent to the Fort Leavenworth Penitentiary in 1912, Strong's granddaughter Thora kidnapped. Charles and Annie Strong hired John Frank Oldfield, the former postal inspector responsible for arresting Perkins and Franklin, to find the girl, and ultimately, Thora was recovered and returned to the Strong family.

The Strong family, especially Annie, was forever in debt to Oldfield for his recovery and safe return of their granddaughter. For Charles Strong, he would remain protective of his granddaughter until his death.

President William Taft photographed at the Strong mansion during his visit to Erie in 1911. *From left to right*: President Taft, Thora Strong Ronalds, Charles Strong, Charles D. Hilles, Thora Ronalds, Annie Strong and Major Archibald Butt. *From the Erie County Historical Society.*

Within the grounds of the Somewhere Estate, Charles Strong never allowed Thora to play with other children. She was forbidden to eat exotic foods, could only speak French and was always accompanied by her bodyguard, Charles Storch. When escorting Thora around the grounds of the estate, Storch was often armed with a pistol and two trained dogs.

Thora was often spotted by other children who visited the estate, particularly Irene Ritter, who remembered, "She looked so lonesome to us."

Charles Strong could also be seen walking alone on the estate. "He was kind of a loner, I think," Ritter later reminisced. "If he'd go by us, he'd nod. Once he tipped his hat at me. I was so thrilled. My aunt told me he did that when he liked you."

Despite their separation, Charles and Annie Strong remained contributors to Hamot Hospital and helped establish the Zem Zem Home for Crippled Children. They continued to engage in many humanitarian acts in Erie, donating land to the Erie County Historical Society and many charities, including the Florence Crittendon Home. The Strongs were also influential in making improvements to Erie's East Canal Basin.

Although Charles was a lifelong registered Republican, he remained independent in politics, was a member of the Episcopal church and was an active supporter of the Erie Day School. A portion of his estate was later gifted to the school.

Charles Hamot Strong died on November 8, 1936, and was interred in the family mausoleum in the Erie Cemetery.

Following the death of Charles Hamot Strong, his Somewhere Estate, then reduced to forty-seven acres, remained overlooking Presque Isle Bay, empty and desolate under the supervision of Strong's longtime secretary, Grace Morton Virture, who oversaw the caretakers of the estate.

The log cabin, Strong's pride and joy, remained abandoned after 1939 and was often vandalized and broken into. The once-bountiful grounds on the estate itself soon were overgrown with shrubbery and dense woodlots. Portions of the estate were sold at auction by the Louis Traiman Auction Company of Philadelphia on December 10, 1969, at the Holiday Inn in downtown Erie. Zurn Industries purchased the property for $525,000, with plans to build a townhouse complex there.

Gradually, the large swaths of land that once belonged to the Strong family disappeared, including the tracts east of the Somewhere Estate between Peninsula Drive and Sommerheim Drive, which were gifted by Strong's granddaughter Thora Ronalds McElroy in 1974.

On September 26, 1975, a permit for the demolition of Charles Strong's cabin was issued by the city. Late City councilman Mario Bagnoni criticized the move by Zurn, claiming Strong's cabin was a city landmark. And he pointed out that Zurn Industries had made promises to retain the cabin for use as a community center.

However, attorney David Lund and architect Richard Wiebel, who represented Zurn Industries, defended the decision: "It's not a specific piece of period architecture," Lund said to the *Erie Daily Times*.

Studies claimed it would take $500,00 to restore the cabin to its former glory. Prior to the demolition, an interior decorator stripped the cabin's interior for salvaging. Some of the objects saved included a gold-lined toilet bowl, hand-hewn stones, wooden beams and other objects.

Despite the outcry and opposition, the demolition of the Strong log cabin commenced.

Charles Strong's Somewhere Estate no longer exists, with the majority of land that was purchased by Zurn Industries now the site of LECOM Bayfront and South Shore Place. Stones and small boulders removed from the log cabin's foundation were used in the construction of the stone wall entrance of the property.

Charles H. Strong reads a book on the porch of his log cabin, which looks over Presque Isle Bay. *From the Erie County Historical Society.*

The Strong mansion remains one of Erie's most iconic examples of historic architecture. After the passing of Annie Strong in 1928 and following the death of Charles, their daughter Thora became the legal owner of the home. Thora, however, lacked any desire to remain in Erie full time and had already moved to New York City years prior, leaving the mansion vacant. Three years after her father passed away, Thora Strong died, passing ownership of the home to her daughter, Thora Ronalds McElroy.

The granddaughter of Charles and Annie Strong was now their last remaining descendant. In March 1941, the Strong mansion was sold to Bishop John Mark Gannon, who sold it to Gannon College four years later. Gannon College later became Gannon University. The Strong mansion is now known as Old Main on campus, where it serves as the administrative offices for the college.

The extortion case against Charles Strong in 1909 remains one of the many stories of Erie's vanishing history, and its sensationalism is the type of a period forever lost.

4

"IF YOU GET HIM, GIVE HIM THE FULL EXTENT OF THE LAW..."

The Phantom Burglar's Reign of Terror

As the city of Erie welcomed 1926, it was closing a door on a year that saw increased criminal activity. Following a chaotic 1924, city officials and local law enforcement authorities expected 1925 to follow in the same chaotic manner.

Crime continued, however, to fester like a gaping wound in the Gem City. In 1925, 8,035 men and women were arrested, 5 homicides were recorded, 67 homes were burglarized and 89 businesses and offices were broken into. The highest increase in crime was the theft of 226 automobiles. There was optimism that 1926 would be a better year.

As December came to an end, though, those in Erie were unprepared for the reign of terror that would encapsulate the city for nearly a month.

The trepidation began on the night of December 26, 1925, when a maid for William C. Varnum, a local salesman, arrived at the Varnum household at 445 West Seventh Street. As she entered the home, the maid discovered several rooms had been ransacked and called the police.

Motorcycle Patrolman William Carney was the first to arrive at the Varnum home, and he inspected the small, two-story family home. Carney discovered entrance to the home was gained through a rear window. Initially, an attempt had been made to break a piece of glass out of the rear door in order to unlock the door from inside, but this appeared to be unsuccessful.

Carney believed the break-in occurred on the evening of December 24, after the family had left to travel out of town. A search of the home revealed nothing of value was missing.

Downtown Erie, looking west. Note the spire of St. Peter's Cathedral, which was near many homes attacked by the Phantom Burglar. *From the Erie County Historical Society.*

Several days later, around 8:30 p.m., on the night of December 29, 1925, Dr. David V. Reinoehl was inside his residence at 139 West Tenth Street when he observed a prowler at the front door attempting to gain access to his home. Reinoehl notified police, and the prowler disappeared. On the floor of the vestibule of his home, Reinoehl found a pair of keys that had been inside his automobile, which was parked inside the garage.

Downtown at police headquarters, Lieutenant Richard J. Dundon detailed Detective Sergeants Stanley Kubeja and Louis Kubeja, along with Patrolman Frank Pfadt to investigate. Soon, the men arrived and began searching outside the home. Detectives later confirmed the prowler had taken the keys from inside Reinoehl's vehicle before attempting to gain entry to the home.

As the officers braved the brittle, cold December air that night, they followed a pair of footprints they believed belonged to the prowler into the backyard and over a rear fence. The trail led to the vicinity of St. Peter's Parochial School on West Eleventh Street, which was where they suddenly vanished.

After the incident at 139 West Tenth Street, police received reports that someone had entered the office of Dr. Edward Dennis at 309 West Tenth

Street and ransacked it before taking off with only thirty-five cents. After police arrived at Dr. Dennis's office, they located evidence that led them to believe the break-in was an attempt to obtain drugs.

On the night of December 31, 1925, thousands of men and women in Erie turned out downtown to celebrate as they welcomed the new year. Around 10:00 p.m., former mayor William J. Stern and his wife returned to their home at 563 West Eighth Street and discovered all the rooms were ransacked. Stern made a brief search and determined nothing had been stolen but still contacted police. Detective Sergeant Kubeja arrived with Patrolmen Frank Pfadt and Robert Holmes.

Police discovered that whoever had broken into Stern's home attempted to jimmy the window before breaking the glass, reaching inside and lifting the window to enter. Under the broken window were a pair of footprints in the soft snow left by a pair of O'Sullivan rubber-heeled shoes, identical to those found at both the Reinoehl and Varnum incidents.

Incredibly, while at the Stern residence, Detective Sergeant Kubeja received a phone call about another break-in that occurred around 10:15 p.m. at the home of Joseph Chojnacki at 736 East Tenth Street.

Kubeja and Pfadt raced to the Chojnacki residence on Erie's east side. At the rear of the home, the burglar had gained access by forcing open the storm door and then smashing the window on the interior door. The Chojnacki family had been away from the home when the incident occurred, and it was later learned nothing was taken from the home. This puzzled Kubeja, because various pieces of expensive jewelry had been passed up, leading him to believe the motive was money.

A substantial amount of blood was found by the broken window of the rear door and inside the home, suggesting the burglar had cut himself when breaking into the home.

Detective Sergeant Kubeja filed his report with his superiors and quietly expressed his concerns about the multiple break-ins that had occurred over the past several days and suggested they may have been committed by the same individual. Others, too, began to see a pattern.

It was not just police who began noticing similarities; the local press was picking up on this.

The *Erie Dispatch Herald* described the next steps the prowler, who worked "like a phantom," took when breaking into the homes: "Breaking a pane of glass to get at the window lock, the burglar has entered each of the four homes in a similar manner. The house is given a thorough ransacking, but in each case police report, that all valuables are left untouched."

A winter darkness familiar to those who live among the Great Lakes returned to Erie, holding its snow-covered streets and homes hostage with uncertainty and growing alarm.

With the paralyzing darkness came more burglaries.

A groggy Louis Cavanaugh returned to his home at 206 East Ninth Street late at night on January 1, 1926, and opened his door to a frightening sight. His home was ransacked by a burglar who went room to room but interestingly enough passed up twenty-five dollars in cash, valuable silverware and a diamond ring.

It was clear the same burglar was responsible.

Occupants of the home were away when the burglar broke the rear storm door window and forced his way through an inner door. As detectives progressed through the home, they observed several windows of the home were wide open, possibly to allow for different routes of escape.

As police were investigating the break-in at Louis Cavanaugh's home, Rudolph C. Liebel returned to his home at 241 East Sixth Street and found his home, too, had been broken into and ransacked. A child's piggy bank with two hundred pennies was reported as missing. Motorcycle Officer Edward Englert and Patrolman Joseph Kubeja arrived at the Liebel home and found evidence consistent with that of the burglaries that had occurred since December 26, 1925.

Police soon became saturated with additional calls of other break-ins throughout the city.

Arthur W. Brevillier discovered the home of his neighbor Dorothea K. Conrad at 630 West Seventeenth Street had been burgled and ransacked. Nothing of value was missing. Edward J. Stark of 315 East Eleventh Street witnessed a man attempting to climb a ladder resting against his home. After being spotted by the Stark family, the burglar jumped from the ladder and disappeared into the night.

Orders were given to all officers and detectives of the City of Erie Police Department to arrest all suspicious persons found loitering or walking the streets in an effort to catch the burglar responsible for the break-ins. Soon, patrolmen were checking dark alleyways and backyards in the hope of catching the burglar in the act.

Despite growing concerns and increased patrols, the burglaries continued.

The residence of John George at 1120 Poplar Street was broken into on the night of January 2, its rooms ransacked. This time, a diamond ring valued at $450, an additional $125, a ruby ring valued at $40, diamond chips valued at $75 and $20 in cash were all taken by the burglar as spoils.

Leslie Potter returned to his home at 258 West Fourth Street that same night around 11:00 p.m., and when he was on the second floor, he spotted a man escaping through an open window in the rear of his home. No valuables were taken, but a photograph was found on the floor of the kitchen. It was unknown if the photograph belonged to Potter or the burglar.

Potter was the first of several to provide a description of the burglar's appearance: a young white male with a slender build standing at about five feet, six inches, tall and dressed in a light overcoat and a light cap.

The burglar struck one more time that night at the home of Edwin C. Schmidt, located at 923 Walnut Street, where he stole one dozen silver knives and forks and half a dozen teaspoons valued at fifty dollars.

In just seven days, over eleven homes had been burglarized and broken into.

On January 3, 1926, the *Erie Dispatch Herald* gave the burglar a name: The Phantom Burglar.

THE O'SULLIVAN-HEELED FIEND STRIKES AGAIN

The Phantom Burglar, who invaded homes in Erie's east and west side neighborhoods, was believed to have acted alone, according to detectives probing the break-ins. The homes that were broken into also provided numerous circumstantial clues, which linked them together.

As he continued to burglarize homes, his MO, or *modus operandi*, continued to evolve. After being spotted by some of the occupants of the homes he broke into, the Phantom began opening numerous windows and doors to allow for many routes of escape if he was cornered.

It was also believed he was not an experienced burglar. He often overlooked many valuable items that an experienced burglar would have noticed. Police also began to notice the Phantom's tendency to enter homes around the West Ninth Street area, believing this suggested a familiarity with the neighborhoods. It was possible the burglar resided in the area or had prior connections that made him comfortable there when engaging in his criminal activities.

The burglaries now attracted the attention of Police Chief William F. Detzel and Lieutenant of Detectives George J. Christoph, who vowed to stop the Phantom Burglar at all costs and bring him to justice.

The evening of January 3 saw six more homes entered by the Phantom Burglar, who worked "with a boldness that smacked of utter disregard for the police."

As the Phantom Burglar trudged from home to home throughout the city unmolested, paranoia heightened among the city's citizens. On one occasion, a homeowner on West Eighteenth Street frantically called police, claiming the Phantom Burglar was inside her home. Police sped to the scene and located a broken window on the side of the house. They later determined an icicle had become dislodged from the roof and struck the window.

On the afternoon of January 4, 1926, police arrested the first of many suspects in the burglaries, twenty-six-year-old Alfonso Curley, a Black man residing at 536 West Twelfth Street. Despite Curley not being the "young white male" described in the papers, he was held and questioned by detectives. Another Black man, twenty-nine-year-old Raymond Butler of 1305 Parade Street, was also arrested as a suspect and taken to police headquarters.

Butler was released just before midnight on January 4, while Curley remained in custody overnight, despite police acknowledging they had no evidence against him for the burglaries. Curley was questioned the following morning by Lieutenant Christoph, while Detective Sergeants Scalise and Kubeja inspected his residence, later reporting there was no evidence suggesting he was the Phantom Burglar. Curley was released later that afternoon.

Edward Kane of 521 Raspberry Street called the police later that evening, claiming attempts had been made to enter his home the day prior. Police arrived and found signs someone had attempted to jimmy the rear window of his home.

They also located footprints made by O'Sullivan heeled shoes.

Shortly after midnight on January 6, 1926, Police Officer Ellsworth Cox was sitting on an eastbound trolley at the intersection of West Fourth and Liberty Streets when a white male wearing a light suit, a light gray overcoat and light cap and carrying a suitcase attempted to board the car. When Cox and the man made eye contact, the man leaped to the ground and fled on food.

Officer Cox, believing the man was up to no good, briefly chased him until he disappeared. Cox immediately alerted headquarters of the incident, and additional officers, led by Detective Sergeants August Heisler and Frank Gaczkowski, flooded the neighborhood to search for the suspicious man.

A thorough search of the west side continued into the early hours of the morning without success.

Fred Blair of 3142 Peach Street was awakened around 1:30 a.m. and discovered a prowler outside. Blair later told police he had previously chased the same man away three times, but he had disappeared into nearby

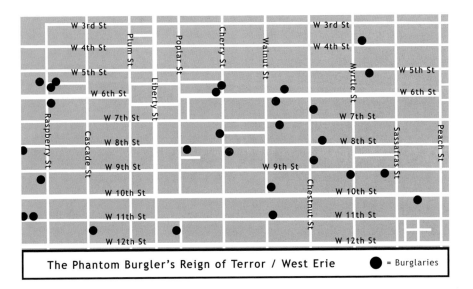

The Phantom Burglar's Reign of Terror / West Erie ● = Burglaries

backyards. Alfred Adams of 744 East Twenty-First Street called police after finding his home had been robbed, but police believed evidence suggested this report was exaggerated.

Until the sun rose that morning, police were hampered with false reports and frightened homeowners. One homeowner was so frightened by the Phantom that when a cat jumped off her windowsill onto the floor, she rushed to the phone and called police.

Police caught a break that morning when a man named Grant Gillespie located a pair of discarded O'Sullivan rubber overshoes stuck in the mud under the window of his home at 1901 Cascade Street. Gillespie told police that the night before, he was awakened by the sound of his two bulldogs barking, and evidence suggested this had scared the Phantom away from his home.

That same night, just after 8:00 p.m. at the home of Arthur B. McDonald at 458 West Eleventh Street, the Phantom Burglar was spotted by a maid as he opened the door on a milk cabinet near the kitchen entrance. As the maid screamed, seeking out McDonald, the Phantom disappeared from the home.

Motorcycle Officer Max Pasky arrived within minutes and tracked the Phantom's footprints through several neighboring yards and then onto West Sixth Street. While tracking these footprints, Pasky also found evidence the Phantom had attempted to enter four nearby residences.

Following the Phantom's trail, Pasky trudged through the snow to West Seventh Street, where the trail ran eastward between two houses the

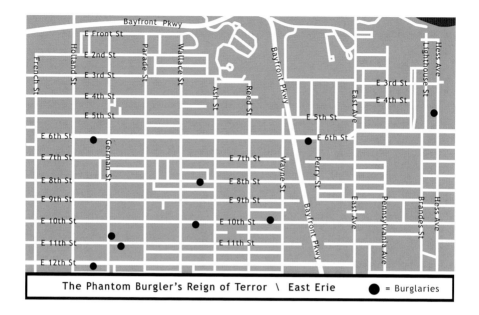

The Phantom Burgler's Reign of Terror \ East Erie ● = Burglaries

Phantom had made additional attempts to enter. From there, the Phantom vaulted over several fences before attempting to gain access to several other homes before exiting onto West Sixth Street near Chestnut Street, where the footprints were lost in the slush. Pasky later reported evidence also led him to believe the Phantom had searched for money left in milk bottles on the doorsteps of homes.

Around 10:00 p.m., Matthew Gleisner of 937 West Twenty-Fifth Street reported to police that his storm door at his home was ripped from its hinges, but he did not believe it was related to the Phantom attacks, chalking it up to someone with a personal vendetta against him.

That week, the City of Erie Police Department had received no less than a dozen reports of prowlers from frightened citizens.

Along with those reports came further arrests.

Twenty-six-year-old Richard Evans, a known floater, was arrested at West Twelfth and Peach Streets on January 7. Evans was well acquainted with the police, and police believed Evans knew something about the recent burglaries. Police also had evidence Evans had been prowling neighborhoods during the prior five or six nights. Held on a charge of suspicion, Evans was questioned the following day by detectives.

Twenty-four-year-old George Wagner of 523 West Second Street was also arrested on the night of January 7 by Detective Sergeant James Baron after being implicated in a burglary that occurred on Shunpike

Road. Wagner confessed to the burglary but denied involvement with the Phantom burglaries.

Another suspect, twenty-eight-year-old Charles Beresford, was arrested by Detective Sergeants Heisler and Gaczkowski during the early morning hours of January 8 after W.H. Buelen of 429 Peach Street accused him of attempting to remove a diamond ring from his finger. Beresford, too, denied involvement in the Phantom attacks.

Between 8:00 p.m. and midnight on January 9, the Phantom returned, entering the homes at 1112 German Street and 249 East Twelfth Street. After he was spotted, the Phantom again eluded capture; however, he left behind more circumstantial evidence confirming his presence there.

On the night of January 10, Millward Thomas was eating dinner with his family at their home at 602 West Sixth Street. After hearing noises emanating from the front of the home, Thomas glanced up and spotted the Phantom Burglar taking off through the front door. Thomas said the Phantom looked more like a small man, no older than a boy. It was reported ten dollars were stolen from a pocketbook.

Later that night, police responded to 549 East Eighth Street following reports of a prowler. The individual responsible, however, fled the area before police arrived.

Police were unable to explain why they had failed to arrest the Phantom as pandemonium continued to spread like wildfire. Frightened homeowners overloaded the switchboard claiming the Phantom Burglar was in their home.

For many, the devious wraith had shed his ghostly shadow into homes all over the city, which was now incensed with fear.

In the days that followed, dozens of loiterers, peeping toms and known prowlers were arrested. After being subjected to a lengthy interrogation, the men were all subjected to an extensive search of their lodgings and personal property. Without any tangible evidence, the men were released, especially when the Phantom's activities continued uninterrupted while those arrested were behind bars.

On the evening of January 12, Edgar and Dorothy Shenk left their home at 446 West Sixth Street around 6:15 p.m. Several minutes later, a maid employed by the Shenk family found the front door open. Believing the Shenks had forgotten to lock the door, she thought nothing of it. After Edgar Shenk and his wife returned home, they discovered Dorothy's mesh purse, valued at $100, was taken from the home.

That same night, Raymond Wallower heard a strange noise coming from his basement at 1402 West Eighth Street. After deciding to inspect

The former location of 235 West Fifth Street, where Dorothy Shenk's discarded purse was found by police. It is one of the many historical sites forever lost to history. *Author's collection.*

the sounds, Wallower spotted a man running from the rear of his basement and then disappearing between a pair of houses north of his home. Police responded and located the footprints of the Phantom under a side window that had a small pane of glass broken underneath the lock.

The day after, around noon, Dorothy Shenk's mesh purse was found discarded alongside a house at 235 West Fifth Street. Police inspected the contents inside the purse and found Dorothy Shenk's driver's cards and personal effects untouched, with only seven dollars in cash missing.

That afternoon, twenty-two-year-old John Trevison was arrested by Detective Sergeants Kubeja and Scalise at the corner of East Eleventh and State Streets. Trevison, who was unemployed and had a criminal record, previously was arrested in 1925 for illegally entering Saint Peter Cathedral and climbing to the top tower, claiming God had instructed him to do so.

Trevison was later questioned by Lieutenant Christoph and held pending further investigation, despite the fact that no evidence tying him to the Phantom Burglar case had been found. He was released the next day.

Throughout the night of January 13, Motorcycle Patrolmen Joseph Kubeja and Edward Englert investigated reports of prowlers in the vicinity of West Eighth and West Ninth Streets, between Sassafras and Myrtle Streets. Very little was discovered aside from several pairs of footprints in the backyards and windows of some of the homes.

January 14, 1926, was the first day in nearly two weeks that a call had not been received for burglaries, attempted break-ins or prowlers. The *Times* proclaimed, "Erie's 'phantom' and 'dinner hour' robbers rested on their laurels last night" when reporting of the uneventful night the following day, an occurrence welcomed by many.

The absence of Erie's Phantom Burglar, nonetheless, was short-lived.

Just after 6:00 p.m. on Friday, January 15, 1926, Georgia Berriman and a friend were just sitting down for dinner at 510 West Seventeenth Street when a loud noise came from the bathroom. As both women left the table to inspect the rear of the home, they captured a glimpse of the Phantom as he dashed through the house. After thrusting open a window, the Phantom jumped from the second story, landed on the porch and escaped.

Police later determined the Phantom had scaled a post on the rear porch and entered through a second-floor window. Patrolmen Frank Pfadt and Julius Talbert also found several fingerprints left behind by the Phantom. Lieutenant Christoph viewed the prints in person and later ordered additional photographs of the fingerprints to be taken.

On January 16, Leroy R. Stevenson returned to his home at 841 East Sixth Street to find the Phantom Burglar inside. After hearing Stevenson enter, the Phantom ran down the stairs and through an open back door. After jumping off the rear porch, the Phantom ran until he tripped on a low wire fence near the alley. Before Stevenson could give chase, the Phantom had picked himself up and escaped. He was last seen running down East Seventh Street.

Officers Pfadt and Holmes located a hole in the glass in the back door of Stevenson's home, which had allowed the Phantom to slip his arm inside and loosen the latch. Stolen were a diamond ring, a loaded revolver and a child's piggy bank containing ten dollars in small coins.

A half hour later, police were called to 1250 Peach Street, the home of Mrs. J. Petrie, who claimed her house had been robbed. A revolver was also missing. Charles Duncon was checking up on his in-laws' residence at 154 Hess Avenue while they were out of town and discovered the home had been broken into. Fifty cents had been taken.

More calls came later that night, and Officer Julius Talbert was detailed to investigate reports of a suspicious man near the corner of West Ninth and Myrtle Streets, where Eugene Haesener of 820 Myrtle Street claimed someone had rung his doorbell and disappeared before he could respond.

Captain Joseph Heard of the Salvation Army returned home from services at 10:30 p.m. on the night of January 17 to find his home at 1314 West Eleventh Street was ransacked and entered. Heard phoned the police and later reported twenty-five dollars in cash and a Christmas present were missing, along with one dollar in cash that had been left on a dressing table.

Charles J. Rapp, Heard's next-door neighbor at 1312 West Eleventh Street, also reported his home had been broken into, with the only item missing being a flashlight. Motorcycle Officer Kubeja responded to both homes and was unable to find any other clues that could lead to the arrest of the Phantom.

On the afternoon of January 18, Detective Sergeants Kubeja and Scalise responded to a vacant lot near the Erie City Iron Works at East Eighth and Perry Streets. There, they located the child's bank stolen from the home of Leroy Stevenson on January 16. Nearby, under a pile of discarded barrels, they found a pair of rubber overshoes believed to have been used by the Phantom to disguise his footprints.

Kubeja and Scalise theorized that on the night of January 16, following the robbery of the Stevenson home, the Phantom traversed two blocks south before discarding his overshoes and the bank and leaving the area.

Despite having fingerprints, eyewitness identification and two pairs of overshoes believed to have been used in the burglaries, which had reached a record number of twenty-five within the city, police were unable to find the Phantom—who continued to remain one step ahead of them.

Emma Walker entered her kitchen at 453 West Sixth Street and saw the face of the Phantom pressed against the glass of a rear window as he attempted to force his way into her home. Upon being discovered, the Phantom fled south, running toward the garage and jumping over the fence in the direction of West Seventh Street. Officers Pfadt and Holmes arrived within several minutes but lost the Phantom's trail.

A short time later, Bertha F. Schaffner of 2815 Holland Street phoned the police after suspecting someone had attempted to enter her home. The prowler ran away when Schaffner's dog scrambled toward a lower floor window.

Faced with the fact that they were no closer to apprehending the Phantom Burglar, detectives culled all evidence in the burglaries and reviewed the case that had occurred since December 26, 1925. A reporter from the *Erie Dispatch* wrote about the status of the investigation after questioning several detectives:

"The phantom is using various means of camouflaging his identity, police learned yesterday. Whereas he started his campaign with O'Sullivan rubber heels, he is now using other footwear on his escapades, charging frequently and abandoning footwear within a short distance of various jobs."

Detective Sergeants Heisler and Gaczkowski continued to make arrests, taking Charles Overpick of Chicago and Thomas Jones of Scranton into custody for suspicious behavior around 2:00 a.m. on January 20 near East Fourteenth and Turnpike Streets.

Later that afternoon, both Overpick and Jones were interrogated at police headquarters and released.

That night, the residence of Frank and Addah Losey, located at 719 Cherry Street, was entered using a pass key, and the entire home was ransacked. But the burglar failed to find $30 in cash, a check for $108 and a valuable gold watch in another room but did obtain $100 in cash and $51 in checks. Addah Losey did not notice the missing items until January 21, when she filed a report with the police.

Detectives and patrolmen for the City of Erie Police Department were struggling to apprehend the Phantom Burglar. It was only during the early morning hours of January 23, 1926, that the Phantom Burglar would add another crime to his rap sheet: murder.

MURDERED AT THE POST OF DUTY

In response to the growing criticism, Chief Detzel ordered a special detail of police officers and detectives to infiltrate the west side neighborhoods in the hopes of catching the Phantom. Just after midnight on January 23, 1926, plainclothes detectives passed through Erie's west side, concealed in alleyways and on porches of homes.

Others, grouped in pairs, patrolled backyards in the hopes of catching the Phantom in the act.

Forty-two-year-old George Greener, a private watchman, was also on patrol that night throughout the neighborhood of West Ninth Street between Myrtle and Chestnut Streets. Greener had been hired by eight families four years before to protect the neighborhood and was always armed with a revolver. After the Phantom Burglar struck in the neighborhood, Greener armed himself with a second revolver in case he should come face to face with the elusive burglar.

George Greener. *From the* Erie Daily Times.

Just after 1:00 a.m., George Greener was standing on the corner of West Ninth and Sassafras Streets, taking in his surroundings. Normally James Powers, a patrolman, would perform his one o'clock pull from the police book at West Eighth and Sassafras Streets before meeting up with Greener, where the two would speak briefly.

That night, James Powers was off duty, and Greener began walking south on Sassafras Street, his feet crunching against the ice and snow as he passed the silent silhouette of Saint Peter's Cathedral. When Greener paused at the corner of West Tenth and Sassafras Streets, he spotted a fresh pair of footprints in the snow heading west on West Tenth Street.

From a distance, Greener looked on as a dark shape, which appeared to be a person, loitered suspiciously before disappearing out of view near the rectory of Saint Peter's Cathedral.

Greener waited several minutes before following in pursuit and concealing himself behind a tree on West Tenth Street, watching from a distance as the suspicious person slipped between two houses and over a wooden fence into the backyard of Dr. David Dennis at 221 West Ninth Street. Greener watched the man break a side window and enter the Dennis residence.

Ensuring he had both of his revolvers, Greener pursued the man, who he was sure was the Phantom Burglar, through the snow and over the fence into the backyard of 221 West Ninth Street. It was only after Greener inspected the broken window that he was certain he was on the trail of the elusive Phantom.

Using a pass key, Greener entered the home, his revolver drawn. His heart throbbed as he breathed heavily, moving from room to room in the home. When he reached the first floor, Greener came face to face with the Phantom, who suddenly rushed into a bathroom at the rear of the home, slamming the door behind him.

Greener was quick to follow as he threw his weight against the door in an attempt to apprehend the Phantom. As Greener struggled to open the door, he failed to see the muzzle of a revolver sticking out, pressed against his body.

The bark of four gunshots reverberated loudly through the narrow hallway with tremendous ferocity, the last bullet entering the right side of Greener's torso, perforating his liver and tearing into his intestines.

Greener released his grip on the bathroom door as he collapsed in the hallway, clutching his stomach.

He caught his last view of the Phantom as the man escaped through a bathroom window.

The gunshots had awakened Dr. Dennis and his wife, Maude, and soon, they thundered down the stairs with alarm, only to find George Greener crumpled on the floor in a pool of blood. Dr. Dennis tended to Greener as his wife called the police.

Within three minutes, Detective Sergeants August Heisler and Frank Gaczkowski arrived, assisted by Motorcycle Officer Andrew Vamos and Patrolmen Paul Luthringer, Frank Pfadt, John Bolan and Anthony Williams. The police, after checking the bathroom, found it empty and saw the Phantom's means of escape was the window.

Detectives spoke softly to Greener, trying to get a statement from him. Alongside him was one of his revolvers, which he claimed was loaded. Detectives later discovered the revolver was not loaded, for reasons that remain unknown.

Officers traveled through the backyard of 221 West Ninth Street and followed the retreating footprints of the Phantom but soon lost track of them

221 West Ninth Street, the home of Dr. David Dennis, is the second home on the left. *From the Erie County Historical Society.*

on West Tenth Street. Reporters later learned the size of the footprints were small, which was unusual for a man.

Police feverously searched through nearby alleys, backyards, porches and homes for any trace of the Phantom Burglar but were unsuccessful.

Once again, the Phantom had vanished into thin air.

After being carried from the Dennis home, George Greener was placed into the back seat of a police cruiser driven by Officer Bolan. As Bolan helped lower Greener onto the back seat, Greener clasped Bolan's hand. "If I die," Greener weakly whispered, "tell the chief I want policemen for my pallbearers."

Bolan soon sped from the scene, bound for Saint Vincent's Hospital.

As detectives investigated 221 West Ninth Street, they received reports that the A.P. Burton and Sons Funeral Home at 352 West Eighth Street had been entered sometime that night and ransacked, although nothing was missing. More reports of prowlers, like one seen near the home of Harry Kessler at 521 West Seventeenth Street, kept officers busy. A set of footprints spotted alongside the home indicated a possible visit by the Phantom.

Before the chaos unfolded at the Dennis residence, police learned the Phantom entered the home of Margaret Sternberg at 817 Chestnut Street and pilfered forty cents, along with a ladies' wristwatch. The next home broken into was that of Catherine Murphy, located 617 Chestnut Street, which was ransacked and five dollars taken from a room where Catherine Murphy and another women had slept just feet away. Before leaving, the Phantom went into the dining room, located off the bedroom, and indulged in a glass of milk and a donut, found partially eaten in the pantry.

After this, the Phantom left the ladies' wristwatch stolen from the Sternberg home behind.

Police believed that the Phantom's next visit that night was the Dennis residence.

At Saint Vincent's Hospital that morning, Drs. Harrison A. Dunn and Orel N. Chaffee consulted each other after inspecting George Greener's vitals and injuries. Both doctors determined Greener's wounds were fatal. Greener's wife, Josephine, kept vigil in his hospital room along with their three sons, nineteen-year-old Edward, fourteen-year-old Willard and thirteen-year-old Oscar. As George Greener continued to fade away, doctors notified the police.

Assistant District Attorney Orson Graham and County Detective Leroy Search arrived at Saint Vincent's Hospital after being notified in the hopes of recording a statement for possible prosecution in the future if the Phantom was ever caught.

St. Vincent's Hospital. *From the Erie County Historical Society.*

Throughout his statement, Greener struggled to speak, weakened from substantial blood loss.

George Greener had only one request when asked by Graham and Search: "If you get him, give him the full extent of the law."

Greener's statement also included a detailed description of the Phantom, which was later provided to the public by the *Erie Daily Times*: "The 'phantom' is 24 or 25 years of age about five feet seven inches tall and weighs between 140 and 145 pounds. He has small feet and last night was wearing a dark coat and dark cap."

That afternoon, Detective Sergeants Brown and Barron arrested twenty-one-year-old James Lyons of Toledo, Ohio, on suspicion of being the Phantom based on his physical description, which matched Greener's statement. After several hours of questioning, Lyons was released when detectives were confident he was innocent.

George Greener died around 5:00 p.m. that afternoon after succumbing to his injuries.

When officer Jack Bolan reported to headquarters later that night for his shift, he learned of Greener's death and passed on Greener's final wishes to Chief Detzel.

As police were inundated with the search for George Greener's killer, a farmer in Fairview alerted police that four summer homes had been broken into, with several revolvers and flashlights missing from the properties. Police confirmed access was gained by someone breaking out a piece of glass from the doors and reaching in to unlock the doors, similar to what was done in the Phantom crimes, but they later concluded the break-ins were committed by someone else.

That night, Dr. O. William Renz performed an autopsy on George Greener's body at Saint Vincent Hospital, confirming Greener died from hemorrhaging and shock. Renz also successfully retrieved the bullet, fired from a .25-caliber revolver, from the left-lower portion of Greener's body.

As darkness again devoured Erie's west side neighborhood on the night of January 23, the special detail of plainclothes detectives and police officers returned and launched an all-out dragnet in an attempt to capture the Phantom. The actions of police that night and into the early morning hours of January 24 netted three more suspects: thirty-eight-year-old James Madden of Buffalo, New York; twenty-six-year-old Richard Evans of Syracuse, New York; and Edward Shaw of Erie.

Local baseball player George Cunningham was also arrested on the afternoon of January 24 by Lieutenant William J. Barron of the New York Central Police Department and Detective Sergeants Brown and Barron of the Erie City Police Department. Cunningham, who resembled the Phantom, was questioned for over an hour before he was released.

After his arrest, Cunningham claimed he was insulted by both of the officers who had arrested him and Lieutenant George Christoph and planned to bring a civil case against the police department after hiring an attorney.

After Greener's death, both the *Erie Daily Times* and the *Erie Dispatch Herald* announced memorial funds for Greener's widow and three sons.

The *Times* issued a compelling plea to the citizens of Erie:

It is as little as the people of Erie can do. The Times *believes they will respond nobly. As George Greener was one of the great mass of our people, one of the best of them in fact, it is fitting that this fund be contributed by the mass and that each one contribute his mite.*

Bring in your contribution without urging. Do not wait to be urged to give towards such a worthy cause.

George Greener lost his life in YOUR service, in protecting YOUR HOMES and YOUR LIVES.

Shall it be said that anyone could not and would not give something for a memorial funds to be presented to his widow.

The Times *places the answer up to the people of Erie. Let them answer.*

The *Dispatch Herald* announced a $250 reward for any person in the city who could provide any information that would lead to the arrest and conviction of the Phantom Burglar.

On January 25, in accordance with Greener's wishes, Chief Detzel announced he would assign six police officers to serve as pallbearers for George Greener's funeral on Wednesday, January 27, beginning at 8:30 a.m., with services held at St. Michael's Church. After the services at St. Michael's, Greener's body was escorted for burial at Trinity Cemetery.

In his column "What D'ye Know?" Erie County sheriff Tom Sterrett, who served with Greener's brother during the Spanish-American War, wrote a stirring response to Greener's murder: "I KNOW though that I shall take a great deal of pleasure in transferring the man who shot George Greener the other night. If ever he is apprehended and convicted."

Sterrett closed his column with his dedication to protecting the city of Erie with the same enthusiasm he displayed during his campaign for sheriff:

> *I KNOW that I told the boys and girls of the* Times *office that the solid gold star they had given me would be a crime deterrent. That I'd go out evenings wearing my gumshoes, and carrying my dark lantern, until I came upon a residence where a burglar was packing the family plate into a bag. Then I'd sneak up upon this former Deputy sheriff, the while throwing back my coat to display the badge which would be evidence I had a much right to be in the house as he had, and when the burglar got a squint at it, and came to realize it was pure gold, he'd drop the family plate and chase me. I'd run right down State street, and over West Fifth, to the jail. The burglar would chase me right on into jail so covetous would he be of that gold star of mine, and all I'd have to do would be to tell Matt Hess to lock him up. Then the crime wave would be over.*

While Sterrett's words promised to bring law and order, an editorial for the *Times* heavily criticized the City of Erie's Police Department and their response to the Phantom Burglar's crimes, which had plagued the city for almost a month :

> *IF the Phantom burglar is to be captured there must be more "pep" in the police department. They must "get on the job."…With the exception of three of four officers there has been practically no extended effort as far as can be seen.…On Saturday of last week George Greener died. It was known early in the morning that he was mortally wounded, but the head of*

the department left his desk at the usual hour in the afternoon 4 p.m. The head of the detective bureau put on his hat and coat and walked out of the station an hour and a half afterwards, to go about his own private affairs until the following day, with the exception of about a half hour Saturday night, which he spent at the station....True some of the plainclothes men worked twenty hours at a stretch on the case. This they did on their own initiative without orders from their superiors. In one instance a plainclothes man sacrificed his day off to work on the Phantom case....But as far as is known not one executive head of the department has put in an hour overtime in an effort to locate the slayer of George Greener. Truly, it is time there was more "pep" in the police department.

The office of Mayor Joseph Williams was also besieged by requests from ordinary citizens to help catch the murderous Phantom Burglar. One such plea came on the afternoon of Tuesday, January 26, when a young boy sat in a chair outside the mayor's office in view of Williams's secretary Robert Clarence Robinson.

Robinson adjusted his glasses, studying the small child, who was slouched in his seat, his coat collar turned up and a cap pulled down over his eyes as he kept his hands concealed deep inside his pockets.

After waiting several minutes, Robinson got up from his desk and approached the youngster, asking him if there was anything he could do for him.

"I gotta see Mayor Williams," the young boy gritted through his teeth with attitude. "I gotta help him catch this here 'Phantom' that's going about the city now robbing and killing people. I'm the boy that can do it and ain't no applesauce or bologna, either!"

At a loss for words, Robinson smiled as he crouched down in front of the boy. "Have you ever been connected with the police? Have you ever done detective work? You see, if you really can catch the 'Phantom,' you're just the fellow the mayor is looking for."

The little boy's eyes sparked as he stood up. "Say, man, ain't you ever heard about me, honest now? I'm an expert on disguises, I am. They can tell you all about me over on Parade Street and how I fooled them all over there when they were having their Mardi Gras celebration. I dressed up like a girl and say I took them all in, I did. They wasn't anybody smart enough to figure me out. I mixed right in with the girls, and they couldn't tell that I wasn't one of them," the boy rattled off, not stopping for air. "I fooled 'em so complete that they put their arms around me and hugged and kissed me right there on the street, and say, I guess that wasn't the apricots for this boy. Oh, I'm smart, I am, mister, on disguises, and I can fool anybody, even that 'Phantom' fellow that's got everybody so scared around here now."

Touched by the boy's tenacity and determination, Robinson thought it was only fair to introduce him to Mayor Williams, which he did several minutes later. Williams listened intently to the small boy's proposition with an "ever-growing twinkle in his eye."

"Yes, I can readily see that you might be able to render the police department a lot of valuable assistance in the present extremity," Mayor Williams said, tapping the boy on the shoulder before kneeling down next to him. "You just go out and keep your eyes open, and if you see anyone you think might really be the 'Phantom,' you just rush to a telephone as quick as you can and let police headquarters know about it."

On Wednesday, January 27, 1926, the funeral services for George Greener began at 9:00 a.m. at St. Michael's Church at the corner of West Seventeenth and Cherry Streets. From there, a long cortege of mourners crawled to Trinity Cemetery. George Greener's widow and three sons, along with dozens of other mourners, looked on as Erie City Police officers Bernard Wilczewski, W.J. Thornton, Oscar Holtz, Anthony Williams, Frank Bolla and Jack Bolan, clad in their dress uniforms, carried Greener's casket to the pit in the earth where he was to be laid to rest.

The repeated failure of the City of Erie Police Department to apprehend the Phantom caused rumors to circulate among the city of a reported shake-up from the mayor's office. Mayor Williams, alarmed at the rising crime wave, had been advised by close friends and those within his department to replace Chief Detzel. Confidence in Detzel, and those under him, was lacking, with police rumored to be demoralized throughout the entire department.

Examples of the frustration from the mayor's office came in the leaks from the police department when Detzel ordered plainclothes detectives into the west side in an attempt to capture the Phantom. Williams's administration believed this tipped off the Phantom, rendering the plan useless.

Following the murder of George Greener, however, the burglaries ceased.

Phone calls to the police continued throughout all hours of the night, with reports that prowlers still haunted the streets and neighborhoods on both the east and west sides. As for the detectives assigned to the Phantom case, they believed the Phantom had left Erie out of fear.

Despite the criticism of the operation of the police department from the *Erie Daily Times*, reporters praised Mayor Williams's work with the department, despite a few mishaps: "He had poor material to work with

The grave site of George Greener in Trinity Cemetery. *Author's collection.*

when he started, but by rewarding the officers who were willing to work and do their duty and shifting those around who were lax in their efforts to stop crime and vice, he has made a wonderful showing."

The *Times* also applauded efforts of those working around the clock to capture the Phantom: "Several individual members of the department are putting forth an almost superhuman effort. These men, loyal officers, are working day and night. They are trying to make the homes of Erie people more secure by stopping this 'Phantom' in his career of thievery and murder."

Mayor Williams decided to bring change to the police department following the murder of George Greener, as pistol practice was announced for officers of the City of Erie Police Department. It was scheduled for February 1 at the ranges of the Keystone Gun Club, located on the third floor of a building on State Street. Practices were scheduled for both the afternoon and evening of the first two weeks of each month until further notice.

The murder of George Greener provided additional tips for detectives to look into and evaluate in the Phantom cases. Several tips pointed to a prior suspect, John Trevison, being responsible for the murder. Despite Trevison being released ten days prior to Greener's murder and cleared of

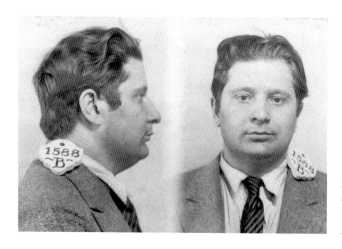

The mug shot of John Trevison from Western Penitentiary. *From the Pennsylvania Archives.*

the burglaries, individuals informed police that Trevison was armed with a .24-caliber automatic revolver and had a tendency to be violent.

Detectives were told to be on the lookout for Trevison and to arrest him if located.

On the afternoon of January 29, 1926, Detective Sergeants August Heisler and Frank Gaczkowski, assisted by Motorcycle Patrolmen Englert and Kubeja, arrested Trevison at the intersection of Eighteenth and Parade Streets. Trevison was held overnight in a jail cell at police headquarters, with plans to question him further the following day.

Trevison was later released. In the future, he would commit further crimes and became known for his violent tendencies. He died at the age of thirty-three at Fairview State Hospital in 1937.

Few robberies occurred in the final days of January, yet police remained unconvinced that the Phantom had returned, wondering if a copycat was now operating within the city.

On the night of January 30, Carl E. Althof, a former officer with the City of Erie, took over Greener's duties as watchman for the East Ninth Street neighborhood after Robert Cruthers, a former New York Central detective, temporarily performed duties as watchman in the neighborhood immediately following Greener's murder.

The *Erie Daily Times*'s George Greener memorial fund was also still going strong by the end of the month. Lester Al Smith of the Colonial Stock Company approached four local theaters managed by the Rowland and Clark Management Company in Erie in an attempt to help raise funds.

Smith visited the Perry, Strand, Colonial and State Theaters and, at each, appeared on stage, where he recited the tragic tale of the heroic George

Greener, who went to his death defending the lives and property of the people of Erie. As he did this, young women from the *Times* passed through the audience to collect funds.

The response was overwhelming, and Smith netted $489 from all four theaters.

County Coroner Dan Hanley announced the inquest into the murder of George Greener was deferred pending further developments, pointing to the fact that detectives were sifting through additional tips and clues in the hopes that some evidence would be found leading to the arrest of the murderer.

A PHANTOM PASSES INTO LEGEND

Though it appeared the Phantom had vanished for good, the paranoia felt by homeowners endured, resulting in an influx of burglar alarm salesmen all over the city. Salesmen also bombarded Mayor Williams's office, hoping to speak with the mayor and Chief Detzel in order to gain their approval.

Erieites like William J. Smead of 19 East Eighteenth Street invented their own burglar alarms. Smead's invention, the "Erie Automatic Burglar Alarm," was tested in the presence of Chief Detzel and regarded as widely successful, with many homes lined up to have Smead's alarm installed.

Palace Hardware House on State Street advertised Smith and Wesson and Iver Johnson revolvers for protection against the Phantom. Mayor Joseph Williams was also approached by a well-known Erie manufacturer who wished to remain anonymous, offering his bloodhounds, free of charge, to apprehend the Phantom.

On the night of February 2, the George Greener Memorial Fund closed, with citizens donating a total of $1,070.59. The *Times* presented a check to George Greener's widow and children the following day.

After a lengthy delay, Coroner Hanley held a coroner's inquest into the murder of George Greener on the night of February 3 at his undertaking parlor, calling five witnesses to provide testimony. The witnesses included Assistant District Attorney Orson Graham, Police Clerk Nicholas Leuschen, Patrolman Alvin Wright, Detective Sergeant August Heisler and Dr. O. William Renz, who performed the autopsy. The coroner's jury rendered the much-expected verdict that watchman George Greener had been shot and killed by a person—or persons—unknown.

Above: An advertisement for the Erie automatic burglar alarm from the February 11, 1926 *Erie Daily Times*. *From the* Erie Daily Times.

Opposite: An advertisement for the Palace Hardware House from the January 25, 1926 *Erie Daily Times*. *From the* Erie Daily Times.

As February faded into March, local newspapers noted that after the Phantom Burglar disappeared from the city, the crime appeared to follow with him. The weeks that followed were relatively quiet, despite several auto thefts and the blowing open of a safe at the United States Laundry at 11 East Fourth Street, where $220 was stolen.

George S. Dougherty, chief of detectives for the New York City Police Department, held a lecture on criminology at the Elks Club, sponsored by the Erie Teachers' Association and the University Club. Dougherty also spoke about the Phantom burglar, comparing his crime spree to cases throughout the country that also remained unsolved, despite the involvement of some of the world's greatest detectives and criminologists: "The Phantom operated at night, under the cover of darkness. It is another lesson in the case of the vain criminal. He derived a lot of enjoyment out of his work because of the newspaper publicity he received," Dougherty told the audience. "Look after the children, correct their faults and see that they are kept in the right environment, and you will be taking a long step in abolishing crime in the United States."

The chilling specter that held Erie hostage was soon forgotten. Soon, the weather gradually turned warmer and wetter. Thousands of naked tree limbs throughout the city accumulated greenery and life, and the days grew prosperous and longer.

It was not until April 7, 1926, that the Phantom case once again captured the interest of the public.

At 3:30 a.m. on April 7, 1926, twenty-four-year-old Leon Massi was arrested by Detective Sergeants Louis Scalise and Stanley Kubeja after he was found hiding in a small steamer trunk inside his home at 1522 Liberty Street.

Massi was one of two individuals believed to have been responsible for the robbery of a drugstore belonging to Raymond Anderson at 10 Clinton Street in the Borough of North East on March 31. After Anderson identified Massi at police headquarters, detectives and officers noticed Massi's appearance was similar to that of the Phantom Burglar and planned to fingerprint Massi to see if his matched those taken from some of the houses that had been broken into by the Phantom.

Detectives also uncovered circumstantial evidence that tied Massi to the Phantom cases, including an instance in which Massi sold a light gray suit to a friend in Buffalo, New York, similar to one worn by the Phantom on several occasions. When interrogated extensively about the Phantom burglaries, Massi shrugged his shoulders and pleaded his ignorance, saying nothing further.

Detectives further consulted with witnesses who saw the Phantom to take part in an identity parade at headquarters. The results of a check of Massi's fingerprints and potential identity parade before witnesses remain unknown to this day.

The mug shot of Leon Massi. *From the Pennsylvania Archives.*

Massi was charged with the theft of $230 in cash and a $1,200 diamond ring. After appearing before Alderman Eugene Alberstadt on April 13, Massi was ordered to be held for trial. Questioned further about the robbery, Massi refused to disclose the name of his accomplice.

The case against Leon Massi began on May 13, 1926, before Judge William E. Hirt at the Erie County Courthouse. Massi was represented by defense attorneys Martin C. Cornell and Jess S. Juliante. Assistant District Attorney Orson J. Graham and R.J. Firman prosecuted the case on behalf of the commonwealth.

The trial was quick and the jury's verdict swift. Massi was found guilty.

On the morning of May 17, 1926, Leon Massi went before Judge Hirt for sentencing. Seated behind Massi in the audience was Massi's pregnant wife and her three-year-old son. Massi's attorneys did not arrive until after the sentencing had concluded. This was said to have been due to a time-sensitive conflict.

Judge Hirt asked Leon Massi if there was anything he wanted to say before sentencing.

"I still maintain my innocence," Massi declared stoically as he stood up.

"That's useless, for the jury has found you guilty," Judge Hirt replied. "Is there anything else you have to say?"

"I have been in jail since April and wish you would be as lenient as possible." Massi pleaded.

"You have been in trouble before," Hirt added.

With a deep sigh, Massi admitted to Judge Hirt that he had been in trouble with the law before, and he admitted to serving eighteen months in Sing-Sing Prison in New York State. Judge Hirt ordered Massi to pay a fine of $200 and serve an indeterminate term of five to ten years in the Western Penitentiary.

Massi's wife wept in court, followed by her young son.

The investigation into the robbery of Raymond Anderson's drugstore in North East continued beyond Massi's conviction and imprisonment, as Detective Sergeants Kubeja and Scalise arrested twenty-two-year-old Frank Costello and questioned him on May 22, 1926, implying he may have been involved in the robbery. A third suspect, Andrew Boccio, was also questioned.

Leon Massi was released from the Western Penitentiary after serving five years. He was arrested again in 1933 in New York City and charged with burglary under the alias Leo Tocci. Massi's luck would run out when his bullet-riddled corpse was fished out of Card Sound on September 25, 1940, north of the Florida Keys. Despite several well-known suspects being questioned, no one was convicted for his murder.

The murder of Leon Massi remains unsolved to this day.

Following Massi's dismissal as a suspect in the Phantom burglaries, mention of the elusive murderer vanished again from both the *Erie Daily Times* and *Erie Dispatch Herald*. The case was not discussed again until December 1926, as the one-year anniversary approached and, with it, rumors that the Phantom Burglar had returned to Erie.

Between 9:30 p.m. on December 10, 1926, and 6:15 p.m. on December 11, 1926, the residence of Charles G. Bryson at 925 French Street was broken into, with every room ransacked. Numerous items were missing, including two overcoats, a full dress suit, a set of studs, two suitcases, three dresses, a set of draperies, a toilet set, a pair of silk pajamas, a pair of teddy bears, a wedding dress and a smoking jacket, totaling $434 in value. When questioning nearby neighbors, police were unable to turn up any further clues.

With the increase in burglaries again, the upcoming one-year anniversary of Phantom Burglar's reign of terror was not lost on investigators.

By December 20, five more home burglaries had been reported. Chief Detzel and Lieutenant George Christoph immediately started taking precautions to curb the rise in home burglaries, which appeared to have started once again.

Fear once again gripped the *Times*'s headline the following day: "SEEK 'PHANTOM' IN TWO THEFTS."

Margaret Kittrell of 427 West Second Street, the wife of a former city policeman, came face to face with a burglar as he ransacked her home around 6:30 p.m. on December 21. When Kittrell started to scream, the burglar fled the home. Police arrived and found that an unlocked window was the point of entry. Unfortunately, Kittrell was unable to provide a description of the man to police.

Patrolman Harry Grant was the second victim that night when his apartment at 124 North Park Row was burglarized while he was on duty and ransacked with nothing stolen.

Police declared another Phantom Burglar was on the prowl in the neighborhoods of Erie. Despite some similarities to the Phantom burglaries from the previous January, police noted other dissimilarities between the two crime sprees, which suggested a possible copycat.

Detectives were later informed of two foiled burglary attempts that occurred during the early morning hours of December 22, 1926. Around 2:00 a.m. at the home of George H. Williamson, located at 438 West Fourth Street, a burglar was scared away when he attempted to remove a window screen, waking members of the Williamson family in the process. An hour later, a prowler unsuccessfully attempted to unlock a door at the home of Charles Erhart at 230 West Twenty-Fourth Street.

In the days that followed, the burglaries suddenly stopped, and the one-year anniversary of the Phantom Burglar's first known crime came and went without incident.

Several days later, the City of Erie welcomed the year 1927. As Chief Detzel submitted his report on crime statistics for the year 1926, only one murder remained unsolved: the murder of George Greener.

The beginning of January 1927 seemed to bring renewed promise to Erie. This changed when nine different homes were broken into during the weekend of January 9 and 10, with a total of $500 taken. Chief Detzel and the Erie City Police Department continued to take extra precautions in an attempt to apprehend the mysterious resurgent burglar who had seemed to haunt Erie's neighborhoods.

The sudden rash of burglaries were followed again by a sprightly silence. Five men were later arrested who appeared to be of suspicious character: Harry Detrick, Otto Schroeder, John Hanley, Walter Ducksworth and William Brooks, all self-proclaimed floaters who claimed they had arrived in Erie several days before from Chicago.

Police got their big break following the recent rash of burglaries on the night of January 23, 1927, when a man attempted to burglarize the Young Women's Christian Association at 130 West Eighth Street. The burglar was confronted by William Weaver, a railroad switchman, and both men became entangled in a struggle when the burglar removed a revolver from his overcoat, with only ten inches separating the men from each other.

The armed burglar pulled the trigger, the bullet narrowly missing Weaver.

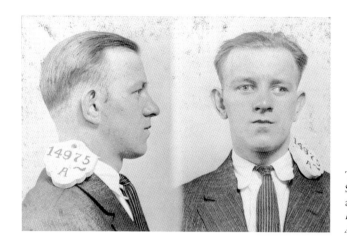

The mug shot of
Stanley Przybywski,
alias Stanley Sibley.
*From the Pennsylvania
Archives.*

Hearing gunshots, Alderman Eugene Alberstadt exited the Elks Club nearby and ran toward the gunshots. When Alberstadt arrived on the scene, Weaver had already apprehended the burglar near the corner of West Eighth and Peach Streets. Soon, several police officers arrived and arrested the man, who gave his name as Stanley Sibley. Officers also recovered a .32-caliber revolver.

When questioned downtown by police, Sibley denied having knowledge of what occurred. It was only after he was grilled extensively a second time that he admitted he had attempted to burglarize the Young Women's Christian Association. Sibley, who had a lengthy past criminal history, also admitted his real name was Stanley Przybywski.

Because of Przybywski's criminal record, police believed Przybywski could have been the Phantom Burglar of 1926. Held without bail, Przybywski proceeded to trial, where he was found guilty of larceny and sentenced to a term of one and a half to three years at the Western State Penitentiary on February 21, 1927.

Przybywski was the last significant suspect in the Phantom cases of 1926. Soon, those cases, along with the unsolved murder of George Greener, joined the collection of cold cases that remain unsolved, and they were soon forgotten as time passed by.

In 1927, there were several occasions when a series of burglaries emerged in Erie, with each burglar earning the chilling moniker "The Phantom."

From February to April 1928, another Phantom Burglar terrorized Erie, followed by separate crime sprees that stretched into the early years of World War II and even afterward into the 1950s. These crimes were accompanied by additional arrests and convictions; however, none matched the fear and intensity of the Phantom Burglar of January 1926.

A PROFILE EMERGES

Although the Phantom was never identified, there is considerable information from the case that can be utilized today. Criminal profiling can help paint a picture of who the Phantom likely was and the type of suspect police should have been looking for.

Evidence suggests the Phantom was a white male aged between sixteen and his late twenties. Eyewitness accounts list him as being of small or medium height with a small shoe size. Those who saw him said he had an "almost boy-like" appearance. He would likely have possessed a prior record consisting of petty theft and would have been known to police. During the course of the Phantom Burglar investigations, detectives or police officers could very well have spoken to the suspect.

Although the Phantom was operating in neighborhoods on both the west and east sides of Erie, evidence suggests he was more comfortable committing his acts within the west side neighborhoods, an area between Poplar and Sassafras Streets bordered by West Fifth and Twelfth Streets.

The Phantom's ability to escape within minutes of the arrival of police supports a personal connection to Erie's west side neighborhoods. It is possible the Phantom lived there at one time during his childhood and currently resided in that area or was employed in the area. When a series of burglaries is perpetrated by a serial burglar, it is believed that the offenses occur within that person's comfort zone, most notably a place of employment or residence. Because of this, the location of the Phantom's first-known burglary at 445 West Seventh Street is of importance.

The burglary at 617 Chestnut Street on the night of January 22, 1926, was one of the most important burglaries committed by the Phantom. Unlike the majority of his burglaries, which appeared rushed and uncomfortable, this burglary suggested the Phantom felt comfortable enough inside the home to indulge in a donut and glass of milk. This suggests the possibility the Phantom personally knew Catherine Murphy or was aware of her habits and lifestyle to the point he knew he would not be interrupted.

Sometimes, the Phantom possessed a jimmy, or a short crowbar used to force open windows and doors, when entering the homes. In other instances, he used a pass key or broke the glass in order to access a latch and enter the home. Evidence suggests the Phantom possessed examples of both an organized and disorganized offender. As his burglaries progressed, the Phantom adapted to different challenges, including, for example, when adjusting to the practice of opening many windows to allow for different routes of escape.

It is likely the Phantom was an amateur when it came to burglary, as suggested by several occurrences when he passed up valuable items in a home. In others, he would steal a considerable amount of coins or paper currency. The burglaries also suggest the Phantom was sloppy in his methods and often engaged in burglaries without premeditation.

The Phantom would have monitored newspaper articles from the *Erie Daily Times* and the *Erie Dispatch Herald*. This would have been fueled by both his paranoia and an attempt to learn any details possible from the investigation. One example is the Phantom utilizing rubber overshoes in an attempt to disguise his footprints after newspapers revealed the brand of shoes that left prints at the burglary sites. The announcement from the City of Erie Police Department that it would have plainclothes detectives enact a dragnet throughout Erie's west side neighborhoods also clearly caused the Phantom to change tactics and engage in burglaries in east side neighborhoods, which he showed a lack of familiarity with.

The murder of George Greener was likely the Phantom's first time committing an act of homicide. It is possible the revolver used in this homicide was one stolen from prior burglaries. The murder of George Greener would have had an incredible effect on the Phantom in the days that followed. If he was employed, he likely would have been noticeably absent from work. It's also likely that he would have changed his appearance or exhibited personality changes that would have been measurable by coworkers, friends and relatives.

After the murder of George Greener, the Phantom's anxiety and paranoia reached a fever pitch, causing him to go into a cooling-off period out of fear of getting caught. This cooling-off period could have lasted for days, weeks or months.

It is possible the Phantom left Erie for some time after the murder, possibly committing similar burglaries elsewhere. It's also possible he was soon arrested in an unrelated incident for in a crime that did not attract attention as being connected to the Phantom case.

As he grew older, the Phantom refined his methods, yet still maintained his signature when he committed burglaries. The Phantom exhibited signs of being a serial burglar and would have only been stopped by a future incarceration or death. It is possible the Phantom committed a later string of burglaries in Erie at a more mature age, decades after the Phantom case had been forgotten.

As for the locations associated with the Phantom Burglar's reign of terror, the home of David Dennis has long disappeared, its exact former location being where a driveway now leads to the north side of St. Peter's Cathedral.

A present-day photograph showing the approximate location of 221 West Ninth Street. *Author's collection.*

Many of the luxurious homes that lined West Ninth Street that horrible January night are also long gone.

Several homes that were burglarized by the Phantom remain. Others are forever lost to history.

Ninety-seven years after George Greener was gunned down in the home of Dr. David Dennis, his murder remains unsolved—one of the twenty-two unsolved murders that occurred in Erie during Prohibition.

The mark of fear left behind by the Phantom is best summarized by a limerick that was sent to the *Erie Dispatch Herald*:

> *There's a phantom lurking in Erie,*
> *Who of policemen and daylight is leery.*
> *He does as he will,*
> *Whether to steal or kill,*
> *He is making all honest folks "skeery."*

5

"HE STEPPED ON THE GAS, AND I KNEW SOMETHING WAS WRONG"

The 1927 Erie County Electric Payroll Holdup

Gus Driggs, treasurer of the Erie County Electric Company, and Ray Pinney, an employee of the company's utility commercial department, left the warmth of their offices at the corner of East Twelfth and French Streets on the morning of September 2, 1927, and climbed into an old Ford coupe. At about 8:40 a.m., the men exited the building and ventured out into the brisk morning on their way to the Second National Bank at West Ninth and Peach Streets.

Arriving minutes later, both men entered the bank. Driggs carried a dark brown satchel underneath his arm. Both men exchanged pleasantries with bank teller Charles Leslie as he filled the satchel with money—$15,103.61, the total for payday at the Erie County Electric Company. With the transaction completed, both men left the bank.

Driggs and Pinney arrived at the East Twelfth Street entrance of the Erie County Electric Company at 8:55 a.m. In 1927, the sidewalk in front of the garage entrance had a considerable bump, which required vehicles entering and leaving to come to an almost complete stop and shift gears to continue.

Pinney turned into the garage entrance, passing over sidewalk before changing gears, causing the vehicle to slow to a crawl when, suddenly, two men, one on each side, appeared and jumped onto the running board of the Ford coupe.

A third man stepped out from inside the garage, standing in front of the vehicle as it lurched to a stop.

All three men were armed with revolvers. Pinney and Driggs raised their hands in the air as the men alongside them pressed the muzzles of their revolvers against their ribs.

"Do you have a gun?" one of the men asked Driggs.

Driggs replied that neither of them were armed, and the man reached in and grabbed the dark brown satchel from between Driggs's feet. And then as quickly as they arrived, the armed men fled and disappeared. Driggs and Pinney remained seated, their hands still raised in the air before they realized the bandits had fled.

Gus Driggs, the treasurer of the Erie County Electric Company. *From the* History of the Erie County Electric Company.

Alexander Brady, an employee of the Erie County Electric Company, was near the garage door when the robbery occurred and watched the bandits dash to an occupied Buick sedan parked against the curb on French Street. When the first of the bandits reached the Buick, the sedan roared to life and peeled off, with the last bandit jumping onto the running board as it turned the corner and disappeared.

In 1956, when interviewed by *Erie Daily Times* reporter Bruce McIntyre, Brady still remembered one of the men had a limp and nearly fell to the ground while getting away.

Detective Sergeants Louis Scalise, August Heisler and William D. Brown of the City of Erie Police Department arrived within minutes and took charge of the investigation. Soon, the case would involve members of the Pennsylvania State Police and Erie County Detectives.

Pinney and Driggs provided police with basic descriptions of the men, which were later printed in the *Erie Dispatch Herald*:

> *The driver of the car was of swarthy complexion and of large build. He was heavily jowled and apparently of Italian parentage. The other three men were of slim build, ranging about five feet, seven inches in height. They wore dark clothes and gray caps. None of the men appeared to be more than 30 years of age.*

William Warden of the Standard Auto Top Company at 1117 French Street witnessed the men bolt to the Buick sedan. Another witness, George

Reese, witnessed the car carrying the bandits peel out onto French Street, where it briefly traveled north before turning east onto East Eleventh Street and then south on Holland Street, where it disappeared out of view.

Also problematic for detectives was that when the robbery occurred in the arched entrance to the garage, this area of the building was twenty feet from the roadway. Unless one stood inside the entrance to the garage, it would have been difficult to observe a robbery taking place.

A night worker from a nearby plant saw three foreign men near the arched entrance to the building around 2:30 a.m., huddled together in deep conversation. When approaching the men on his way to a lunch car at Twelfth and State Streets, he noticed the men terminated their conversations until he passed by. When he returned a short time later, the men were gone.

Detectives believed the two men who jumped onto the running board of the Ford coupe approached the vehicle prior to it reaching the garage entrance. One came from the north on French Street, and the other came from the south. It was clear the men, who were experienced, timed their movements to approach the vehicle as it entered the garage, another indication of extensive preplanning. They also were likely aware Pinney and Driggs were not armed prior to the holdup.

Employees of the Erie County Electric Company mingled with detectives and officers, as they remained at the scene without much other evidence to go on. Detectives also learned the money issued by the bank was given in one- to twenty-dollar bills, which would make it nearly impossible to trace.

Detectives turned to the getaway vehicle, a Buick sedan with an Illinois license plate. Police were aware that a local man, Thomas Brown of 720 Parade Street, reported a similar sedan had been stolen the night before. An alert was put out in search of the Buick sedan. Despite possible sightings of

The Second National Bank. *From the Erie County Historical Society.*

The office of the Erie County Electric Company at the corner of West Twelfth and French Streets. *From the* History of the Erie County Electric Company.

the vehicle, police were left with few clues by noon, when Lieutenant George Christoph spoke briefly to reporters.

Around 1:00 p.m., Detective Sergeant Scalise received a call from the landlady at 1601 Peach Street, informing him that two of the men who boarded at the home were leaving in a vehicle that matched the missing sedan's description. Scalise was acquainted with the landlady and her four tenants due to an incident that occurred several weeks prior when Scalise was making his rounds near West Sixteenth and Peach Streets and spotted four suspicious-looking men.

After enlisting the help of local informants to tail the men, Scalise was contacted by the landlady of 1601 Peach Street. She confirmed she had been renting a room to the four men; however, she could not conclusively provide any tangible details about them or what they were doing in Erie.

Scalise, along with Detective Sergeants Brown and Heisler, jumped into a Cadillac police cruiser and sped toward 1601 Peach Street. Minutes later, the men arrived at the boardinghouse but were too late.

The four suspicious boarders were gone.

Scalise, Brown and Heisler decided to search the nearby neighborhoods for the "loud" red and black Ford coupe with a New York license plate. When traveling on Peach Street, one of the detectives spotted the Ford coupe and immediately turned around and gave pursuit. The Ford accelerated, cutting street corners in an attempt to evade the detectives, peeling rubber as it

A purported sketch of the Erie County Electric Company holdup. *From the* Erie Dispatch-Herald.

reached the intersection of West Eighteenth and Myrtle Streets, where a tire exploded, causing the car to lose control and come to a stop.

Two men, one who appeared to be limping, jumped from the vehicle and fled on foot through the neighborhood.

Scalise and Heisler pursued the men on foot, while Brown drove the detective car around the block in an attempt to possibly cut them off. Within minutes, Scalise caught up to the limping man as he ducked between two houses. The two briefly tussled with each other before Scalise pulled out his revolver and pressed it against the man's face.

The limping man threw his hands up and surrendered as Scalise pushed him up against the wall and handcuffed him. The other man, however, vanished and was last seen in the vicinity of the Erie Paper Box Company at 251 West Nineteenth Street, where employees saw a man matching his description carrying something wrapped in newspaper.

The Cadillac police cruiser screeched to a halt as Detective Sergeant Brown jumped out to assist Scalise and Detective Heisler arrived by foot on scene. Before the limping man was placed into the back seat of the

West Eighteenth and Myrtle Streets, where the sensational car case ended and Salvatore Frangiamore was apprehended after a brief foot chase. *Author's collection.*

cruiser, Scalise grabbed two sets of coats the man had been carrying and briefly inspecting the contents of the pockets of one of the coats, where he located a driver's license for twenty-one-year-old Anthony Palisano of Buffalo, New York.

Scalise immediately put out an alert for Palisano.

At headquarters, the limping man was identified as twenty-year-old Salvatore "Sam" Frangiamore. Frangiamore, who resided in Buffalo, was known by his alias Sam Frenchmore and was employed as a boxer's trainer.

When interrogated, Frangiamore denied his involvement in the crime and claimed he was not in Erie when the holdup happened, claiming he had only arrived in Erie with another gentleman just minutes prior to his arrest and told detectives he was in Erie so he could be present for a boxing match. "I was walking out [West Eighteenth Street] to visit a friend when this guy in a Ford hailed me just past Peach [Street]. I know him by sight, but I don't know his name. He offered me a ride," Frangiamore said to detectives. "All of a sudden, he stepped on the gas, and I knew something was wrong. Then he had the blow-out, and he yelled, 'Run!' I decided I'd better run."

Frangiamore was asked about his relationship with Palisano, the suspected owner of one of the coats he was carrying.

Frangiamore shrugged, insisting Palisano was a stranger to him, although Palisano was later identified by detectives as the second man who fled the fleeting Ford vehicle. Detectives also later learned Palisano borrowed the Ford coupe from a man in Buffalo. When quizzed about the driver of the Ford, Frangiamore admitted the other driver had been carrying a bundle but continued denying knowledge of the contents.

Remembering the incident several weeks prior with the four suspicious men near West Sixteenth and Peach Streets, Scalise was fairly certain that two of the suspicious men were Frangiamore and Palisano.

Gus Driggs and Ray Pinney arrived at police headquarters, where Frangiamore was placed in a line-up.

Driggs, initially unsure at first, identified Frangiamore as the gunman who hid inside the garage and stepped out in front of the vehicle. When presented with a photograph of Palisano, Driggs said he resembled the man who pressed his revolver against his ribs. Pinney could positively identify only Frangiamore.

Despite Frangiamore's denial, there was more circumstantial evidence that suggested he was lying. A key found on Frangiamore after his arrest matched the key to one of the rooms at 1601 Peach Street. Frangiamore insisted it came from Palisano's coat, not his.

Another man, E.A. Pearsall, a boarder at 1601 Peach Street, confirmed that on the morning of the robbery, when he left his room and walked down the hall, he spotted three or four men, one of whom was carrying a package, entering another room.

The mug shot of Salvatore "Sam" Frangiamore. *From the Pennsylvania Archives.*

As one of the men fought to unlock the door, another member of the group spotted the gawking Pearsall. "What in the hell are you looking at?" the man wailed at Pearsall before he hurried away.

Detectives spoke with authorities in Buffalo and learned Frangiamore had a minor record, which included rape. Palisano, listed as a truck driver, possessed a minor record for disorderly conduct.

Despite police believing that Frangiamore and Palisano were involved in the holdup, there was still work to be done in locating the other two men. Detective Sergeant Scalise later learned the third man was likely Daniel "Danny" Sansanese and the fourth man was an individual named Nichola Demarco, alias DeMark. Both of them were also from Buffalo.

Sansanese was born in Buffalo, New York, the son of Sicilian immigrants and began his life of crime at the age of thirteen when he was arrested for grand larceny. In March 1927, he was arrested for vagrancy and later identified as being responsible for several robberies that occurred in Buffalo. Sansanese, held on an open charge for those crimes, was released due to a lack of evidence.

In May 1927, Sansanese and an accomplice in the holdup of Dambach's drugstore in Buffalo and engaged in a shoot-out with police. Sansanese was wounded when he was shot in the back and later spent a month recuperating at Columbus Hospital. When Sansanese became a suspect, he was already being held for trial in Buffalo and was not able to be extradited.

Demarco, the fourth man suspected by police, remains a murky figure, as not much information was released by police about him.

As detectives searched for the three other men, Frangiamore was arraigned before Second Ward Alderman Fred Schmidt and ordered to be held without bail.

A preliminary hearing was scheduled for the following week.

The next morning, police located the Buick sedan used in the robbery, abandoned on Walnut Street between West Eighteenth and Nineteenth Streets. The Buick was the same vehicle reported stolen on the night of September 1. The license plates found on the vehicle were traced to a man named Walter Hannold of Kane, Pennsylvania. To detectives, it appeared the bandits had switched out the license plates on the vehicle in an attempt to evade capture.

Despite intensive interrogations, Frangiamore continued to deny his involvement in the robbery.

Friends of Frangiamore arrived on Sunday, September 4, from Buffalo and retained disgraced ex-mayor and local defense attorney Miles B. Kitts to represent Frangiamore. Kitts immediately plotted Frangiamore's defense, making preparations to have bail fixed. Lieutenant Christoph and District Attorney Davis planned to ask for a high bail amount to be fixed considering the circumstances of the crime.

Several days later, detectives hit a brick wall and were unable to locate the stolen money, although more arrests in the future were rumored.

On September 6, the *Erie Daily Times* called for swift justice:

> *There has been an epidemic of payroll robberies throughout the country. Erie has been an exception to this during the past five years but it was coming. It took place to the tune of $15,000. In crookdom, this is a good job—more so because no one was killed. But that was accidental. The robbers were not threatened and would have killed had they been cornered....They should be dealt with as murderous and bandits.*

On Wednesday, September 7, as Frangiamore's friends and associates demanded his freedom, Judge William E. Hirt decided the serious circumstances surrounding Frangiamore's role in the robbery warranted continued detention, fixing a heavy bail of $10,000. Unable to post bail, Frangiamore was remitted back to the county jail, with his friends promising they would return and provide funds for his release.

Authorities quietly continued the robbery investigation, this time in Buffalo, New York, where they believed the majority of the stolen money would be likely recovered.

The arrest warrant for Anthony Palisano issued by Alderman Fred Schmidt remained.

On September 15, authorities announced the arrest of twenty-five-year-old Tony "Baby Face" Palmisano of Buffalo, New York, who was brought in the day before and detained as a suspect in the robbery. Palmisano's arrest came after a photograph identification was confirmed by Gus Driggs and Ray Pinney.

Shortly after the robbery, Palmisano was placed under surveillance by Buffalo authorities after a request had been placed by Lieutenant Christoph. Palmisano had recently been released from a prison in Auburn, New York, where he had served eight years for burglarizing a post office and bank in Randolph, New York. The day before the arrest, both Lieutenant Christoph and Detective Sergeant William D. Brown traveled to Buffalo to assist police.

District Attorney M. Levant Davis was notified of the arrest and told to immediately started the extradition process. Because of the arrest,

Frangiamore's hearing before Alderman Schmidt was postponed to September 30. Frangiamore posted $10,000 bond on Tuesday, September 20, and walked out of the Erie County Jail a free man as the district attorney's office planned for Palmisano's return to Erie.

Tony Palmisano, however, planned to fight extradition, claiming he was a victim of mistaken identity. The man detectives from Erie had been searching for was Anthony Palisano, Palmisano's attorneys argued. This, coupled with the failure to receive extradition papers on September 30, forced another delay in the payroll robbery case.

On October 11 at an extradition hearing in Albany, New York, Governor Alfred E. Smith refused to sign papers for the extradition of Tony Palmisano based on filings from Palmisano's attorneys that claimed Palmisano was never identified as one of the men wanted in the payroll robbery. Present at the trial, alongside Lieutenant Christoph, District Attorney Davis requested Smith's office to consent to a review of the case the following Monday so Davis could present witnesses in Albany to identify Palmisano.

While Davis and Christoph gathered witnesses for the following week in Albany, New York, Salvatore Frangiamore was bound over to the November term of court on Friday, October 14, by Alderman Schmidt following his preliminary hearing. Frangiamore was represented by defense attorneys Miles B. Kitts and Edward Murphy. The main witnesses providing testimony were Gus Driggs and Ray Pinney. Additional witnesses included Alexander Brady, Lieutenant George Christoph and Detective Sergeant Louis Scalise.

At the additional extradition hearing on Monday, October 17, Governor Smith again refused to grant extradition of Tony "Baby Face" Palmisano, declaring Palmisano's defense attorneys were correct that he had not been positively identified as being involved in the robbery.

Palmisano was released from custody and immediately returned to Buffalo, New York.

Having to retrace their steps, City of Erie Police detectives continued to search for Anthony Palisano. Salvatore Frangiamore's days of freedom, too, came to an end and he was returned to the Erie County Jail after defaulting on his $10,000 bail.

On Monday, November 7, Frangiamore was indicted by the November grand jury.

Several days later, Anthony Palisano was arrested by Buffalo police in Buffalo, New York. Hearing of Palisano's arrest, Lieutenant Christoph informed Buffalo authorities that both Gus Driggs and Ray Pinney

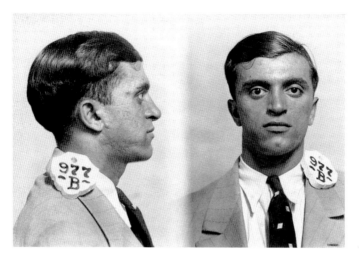

The mug shot of Anthony Palisano. *From the Pennsylvania Archives.*

conclusively identified Palisano as being one of the men involved in the payroll robbery after being shown his photograph.

Detectives departed for Buffalo the following day, and Gus Driggs visibly identified Palisano as being involved in the payroll robbery.

Interrogated by authorities in Buffalo, Palisano confessed to his role in the payroll robbery and named nineteen-year-old Daniel Sansanese as an accomplice. Detectives in Erie learned that he had been found guilty in his trial and given a substantial prison term at Auburn Prison. Palisano also confirmed the involvement of Frangiamore but refused to identify the fourth individual involved.

On November 17, District Attorney M. Levant Davis informed reporters he was still awaiting a response regarding the extradition paperwork for Anthony Palisano and appeared optimistic they would move forward to trial the following week.

Several days later, however, on November 21, 1927, District Attorney Davis announced the postponement of the trial against Frangiamore and Palisano due to the delay in receiving Palisano's extradition paperwork from Harrisburg. Because Davis preferred to try both men together, he decided it would be best to postpone the trial until the February term of court in 1928.

On November 26, the extradition papers were forwarded to New York governor Al Smith for his signature.

In early December, Lieutenant Christoph was notified that the extradition of Anthony Palisano had been granted. Detective Sergeant Heisler left Erie for Buffalo on the morning of December 6 and returned to Erie that afternoon with Palisano in handcuffs.

After his arrival in Erie, Palisano was taken to police headquarters, where he was again interrogated; however, this time, he denied any involvement in the payroll robbery but implicated Salvatore Frangiamore as one of the men involved. "They borrowed my automobile from me in Buffalo to pull the job," Palisano claimed.

"Who do you mean by *they*?" Christoph quizzed Palisano curiously.

"I will make a statement to the district attorney," Palisano responded, refusing to elaborate.

Palisano and Frangiamore remained incarcerated as they awaited their upcoming trial, and Erie soon welcomed the year 1928. In anticipation of the upcoming trial, authorities were widely praised for solving five murders, in addition to the payroll robbery case, in 1927. On top of that, 1927 had seen a decrease in highway robberies and home burglaries and an increase in recovering stolen automobiles. For many in Erie, there was a reason to be optimistic for the future.

Bail in the amount of $10,000 was finally furnished for Salvatore Frangiamore on the morning of Tuesday, January 17, 1928. Following his release from the Erie County Jail, Frenchmore left for Buffalo, New York, where he planned to gather witnesses for his defense. Frangiamore's defense attorney Miles B. Kitts also left for Buffalo to assist in preparation for the upcoming defense.

Rumors continued to swirl about the other two men accused of being suspects in the payroll robbery, claiming incorrectly that one had still been incarcerated at Sing-Sing Prison while the others' whereabouts were unknown after he jumped bail while awaiting trial in Niagara Falls.

Just as the February term of court for 1928 opened, the case against Salvatore Frangiamore and Anthony Palisano was again postponed to the May term of court due to the illness of Miles Kitts.

As for Palisano and Frangiamore, both men were convinced they would walk free.

"I Guess I'll Take a Ride from What She Said"

Salvatore Frangiamore, who enjoyed his freedom while he was out on bond, returned to Erie on Saturday, May 19, 1928, for his upcoming trial, which was to be held the following Monday, where he would be represented by local defense attorneys Miles B. Kitts and Edward Murphy. Local defense attorney Samuel Y. Rossiter represented Palisano.

The defense attorneys for Frangiamore and Palisano attempted to have both men tried separately, due in part to statements made by Palisano not in the presence of Frangiamore, which they claimed could harm Frangiamore's defense.

Judge Uriah P. Rossiter refused the motion, and on Tuesday, May 22, 1928, the case opened in the Erie County Court of Common Pleas and was expected to last throughout the following day. An extensive list of witnesses had been collected for the trial, and for some who could not appear, such as two witnesses from Buffalo, New York, depositions had already taken place that previous Saturday.

After a jury was empaneled, the court was adjourned until 1:30 p.m., when the first of several witnesses took the stand to present their testimony; however, only Gus Driggs and Ray Pinney would be called that day, with Gus Driggs testifying for a substantial amount of time that afternoon.

Unexpectedly, the trial, which had started off sluggishly, was delayed until the following day, Thursday, when Judge Rossiter announced he would be attending the funeral of a close friend, Edward Heartwell, the late president of the First National Bank of Painesville, Ohio. Before excusing jurors for the day, Judge Rossiter cautioned them not to talk with anyone outside of the courthouse about the case. He also said he could have taken them to a hotel to protect the legitimacy of the jury panel but believed this was not necessary.

When court resumed on Thursday, May 24, Attorney Edward Murphy cross-examined Ray Pinney on the stand in an attempt to discredit his testimony, saying that when the holdup occurred, he had only "a fleeting glimpse of" Frangiamore and that the identification was not reliable. Murphy also pointed out that Pinney was unable to conclusively identify Palisano as being present at the scene of the holdup.

The jury sat on the edge of their seats throughout the riveting testimony, which showed the holdup itself lasted only thirty seconds. Murphy focused on this key detail, claiming that both Pinney and Driggs were clearly frightened and did not conclusively get a definitive view of the bandits, all within thirty seconds. This was supported, Murphy claimed, by Pinney's own testimony, in which he claimed the hair of one of the men was dark yet could not recall the color of one of the men's eyes or the color of their suits.

Alexander Brady, who had been standing near the garage entrance, testified that he did not witness the actual holdup occur but saw a man cross the street to a closed car with a black bag in his hand, walking with a limp. District Attorney Otto Herbst pointed out that Frangiamore walked with a limp.

Detective Sergeant Louis Scalise testified about the events that followed the robbery and the arrest of Frangiamore, confirming Frangiamore fought with him before he was subdued.

Following the testimony that afternoon, one of the jurors, Julius Buseck, asked for permission to step outside of the courtroom.

Buseck soon stepped out of the courtroom. A few minutes after Buseck stepped out of the courtroom, Frangiamore followed, and within a few minutes, he followed Buseck into another room in the courthouse, where he attempted to discuss the case within earshot of a court attaché.

At the end of the session for that day, the matter was reported to District Attorney Otto Herbst, who notified Judge Rossiter. Buseck was brought before Judge Rossiter and Herbst to tell his story truthfully before the bench, confirming Frangiamore had followed him and attempted to discuss the case.

After Herbst confirmed Frangiamore attempted to tamper with members of the jury, he submitted the conversation before Judge Rossiter as grounds for discontinuing the trial until the September term of court. Attorneys Rossiter, Kitts and Murphy questioned Buseck in open court and waived their examination, agreeing to the continuance.

Herbst reported the incident to the *Times*:

> *I noticed Frenchmore when he left the room and I became suspicious as did the court. After an investigation, I learned that Frenchmore had spoken to Buseck. Mr. Buseck is a fine gentleman and I'm sure he would not have listened to Frenchmore very long….However, if Frenchmore had the nerve to accost a juror almost directly in the face of the court, I can imagine what has been going on outside. It was for that reason that I asked for a continuance of the case.*

After members of the jury were dismissed, Frangiamore was ordered to return to the Erie County Jail after Judge Rossiter ordered his bail be increased to $15,000.

Anthony Palisano later furnished $10,000 bail on Friday, June 1, 1928. When entering the clerk of court's office to sign a bond, Palisano was so nervous he was unable to write. "It's wonderful to think I'm getting out after seven months in jail," Palisano smirked.

When asked about the holdup, Palisano proclaimed his innocence and said that the whole ordeal was nothing more than a case of mistaken identity.

On Wednesday, June 6, Leonard Pasqualicchio, the president of the Bank of Italy, furnished Frangiamore's bail for $15,000. Despite Pasqualicchio posting the amount needed for bail, Erie County judge William E. Hirt refused Frangiamore's release until Judge Rossiter returned from Philadelphia, where he had been presiding in court, stating that it should be up to Rossiter to decide.

Frangiamore was granted his release several days later on Monday, June 11, 1928.

With both Palisano and Frangiamore free as they awaited their trial, District Attorney Herbst announced a trial date of September 17, 1928.

The long-delayed trial began on Monday, September 17, 1928, before Judge Uriah P. Rossiter. That morning was devoted to drawing a jury, with roughly forty-five jurors having been called before noon and each side exhausting their allowed challenges.

Attorneys for Frangiamore and Palisano prepared for twenty character witnesses to be called from Buffalo, New York, to testify for both men. It was rumored that around roughly thirty-five witnesses in total would be heard and that both sides hoped to wrap up before the upcoming Thursday. Due to the importance of the case and because of what occurred in May, Judge Rossiter ordered members of the jury to be taken to hotels at night during the trial.

Reporters wrote Frangiamore was "an attractive young man, neat in appearance and shows marks of having received a fair education." As for Palisano, he was the opposite of Frangiamore, looking "hard in appearance" and not presenting "the neat appearance displayed by Sam [Frangiamore]."

Soon, a full jury was empaneled, with eight women and four men, and the commonwealth presented its opening arguments.

That afternoon, Gus Driggs was the first witness to take the stand and testified that he recognized both Frangiamore and Palisano as two of the men who took part in the holdup. Ray Pinney, the second witness called, testified he could identify only Frangiamore.

Alexander Brady, who observed one of the bandits limping and carrying the satchel full of money, provided strong evidence against Frangiamore and Palisano and withstood a blistering cross-examination.

The following day, Tuesday, George Christoph, the captain of detectives, testified that when Frangiamore was arrested, his ankle was bandaged. When asked about the injury, Frangiamore told detectives he had sprained his ankle. Detective Sergeant Louis Scalise, who arrested Frangiamore, testified Frangiamore had a limp when he was arrested.

Detective Sergeant Heisler confirmed he could not positively identify Palisano as being one of the men who fled from the Ford coupe after the tire blew out. E.H. Pearsoll, the boarder at 1601 Peach Street at the time of the holdup, testified he rented rooms to three men but could not positively identify Frangiamore and Palisano as being two of the men who had rented the rooms from him. When questioned at length by Judger Rossiter, Pearsoll grew indignant and repeated the same assertions.

Frank Scalise, a cousin of Detective Sergeant Louis Scalise, testified he spotted Frangiamore in downtown Erie near West Sixteenth and Peach Streets after the robbery. Patrol Officer James Yaple testified to the contents found in the coats when Frangiamore was arrested, including a key to a room at 1601 Peach Street.

By the afternoon, the commonwealth had rested, and defense attorneys for both Frangiamore and Palisano opened for the defense.

Frangiamore testified on his own behalf. When asked by his attorney Miles B. Kitts if he was a member of the bandits responsible for robbing Gus Driggs and Ray Pinney, Frangiamore was emphatic in his response. "I absolutely was not," Frangiamore said, looking to the jury.

> *I was not in that territory at the time the robbery is said to have taken place. I got up about 6:30 that day. I was living at 471 Seventh Street, Buffalo, New York, at the time. I went over to Bobby Tracey's house, for whom I worked, and gave him a rub down. Burt Finch, his manager, was also there, as was Tracey's wife. We left Tracey's house about 8:40 and went to a drugstore in that vicinity, where I purchased a few cigars. After that, I went to a barbershop, where I was shaved. It was then about 9:30 a.m.*

Frangiamore continued his testimony, claiming he met a friend, Joseph Jimbroney, who was traveling to Cleveland. Frangiamore asked Jimbroney if he could ride with him as far as Erie, as he wanted to attend a boxing match scheduled in the city that night. Jimbroney agreed to give him a ride, according to Frangiamore. "We left Buffalo about 9:45 a.m. and stopped in Fredonia for a while with a friend and then come on to Erie. I got out on Eighteenth and State Streets at exactly 12:45 p.m."

Frangiamore testified that as he walked west on Eighteenth Street, he reached the intersection with Sassafras Street when a man driving a red Ford coupe called out to him. Frangiamore had seen the man before but did not know his name, yet he accepted the ride from him, telling the man he was heading for Fourteenth and Hickory Streets to visit a friend. The Ford coupe then stopped at 1601 Peach Street, and the driver entered the building, returning a short time later with a package.

When asked if he knew about the contents of the package, Frangiamore claimed he did not know.

The driver started the ignition for the Ford coupe, and the men proceeded on West Eighteenth Street when, suddenly, the driver became nervous and proceeded to "step on the gas."

Several minutes later, according to Frangiamore, the male driver told Frangiamore to run. Grabbing his coat and the other man's by mistake, Frangiamore ran and was soon arrested.

When asked about the key to a room at 1601 Peach Street found in his possession, Frangiamore claimed the key was from the coat that belonged to the unknown man, which he scooped up by mistake before fleeing the auto. Frangiamore also denied having a sprained ankle, claiming that he would not have been able to run from detectives had this been true. This testimony, of course, conflicted with that of George Christoph and others, who confirmed Frangiamore's ankle was bandaged at the time of his arrest.

When District Attorney Herbst cross-examined Frangiamore, he punctured Frangiamore's "perfect alibi." For example, when asked about his sprained ankle, Frangiamore later admitted that his ankle was in fact sprained and bandaged the day he was arrested. Herbst then engaged in a blistering attack on Frangiamore's testimony, reducing the testimony to nothing more than unsubstantiated comments.

Following Frangiamore's testimony, character witnesses from Buffalo testified, corroborating Frangiamore's claims he was in Buffalo and saying that they had seen him there at the time of the robbery. Meanwhile, others testified to the decency of his character.

Character witnesses also testified on behalf of Anthony Palisano, including a boardinghouse keeper on East Sixth Street who claimed Palisano was in his room at Sixth and Holland Streets when the holdup occurred and that he had not left his room until 10:00 a.m.

Spectators who viewed the trial as the defense came to a close felt that the case against Palisano was the weaker of the two, with the strongest evidence being against Frangiamore.

District Attorney Otto Herbst, however, argued for and won permission to reopen his case on the grounds that new evidence had come into his possession. Herbst had one more surprise up his sleeve for Frangiamore and Palisano's defense attorneys when he called fourteen-year-old Ruth Woods to the stand to testify as a witness.

Woods, a waitress from Pittsburgh, testified she met Palisano, who was using the alias "Jack Long," near Pittsburgh roughly a month after the robbery. Palisano, Woods claimed, bragged about his part in the payroll robbery, in which he received $4,000, and celebrated his success by spending money on women.

Palisano and Woods soon ran away to West Virginia. In time, Woods became frightened of Palisano; however, he was too afraid to leave him after he began to threaten her, sometimes with a pistol. "I'll choke you and throw you in the river," Woods claimed Palisano would say to her.

It was only after Palisano and Woods traveled to Wheeling, West Virginia, that Palisano attempted to force Woods into prostitution. Soon, the pair broke up, and Palisano returned to Buffalo, where he was soon arrested.

The jury received the case at 11:10 a.m.

The men and women who had crowded the spectator seats remained seated in the hopes of being present for the verdict. Many of them resorted to eating their lunches in the courtroom. Palisano and Frangiamore expressed confidence that they would be acquitted of the crime. "I'm not worrying," Palisano joked to those around him. "The jurors look like a good bunch. You don't see any gray hairs on my head, do you? Well, I had plenty of time to get them when I was in the jail for seven months before I got bail. I ought to know if I'm guilty or not. That lousy dame from Pittsburgh sealed me, I guess."

Palisano curled his lips around his cigarette, exhaling smoke as he continued, realizing the possibility that he faced jail time. "I guess I'll take a ride from what she said."

Palisano's endless gaze was restored with his trademark smirk as he flicked his wrist, looking to a nearby reporter. "Say, you've got a nice jail here," Palisano responded with a quick puff from his cigarette. "Matt Hess is a dandy guy. I raised plenty of rough house while I was over there, but he didn't say much. Lots of places, they'd have thrown me in a padded cell."

By 3:00 p.m., the jury announced they had reached a verdict.

Sheriff Thomas Sterrett had four deputies in the courtroom when the verdict was read. As the clerk read the verdict, both Frangiamore and Palisano remained motionless.

Both men were found guilty.

Judge Rossiter deferred sentencing pending the filing of a motion for a new trial the following day from both Frangiamore and Palisano's attorneys before ordering both men to be removed to the Erie County Jail.

As Deputy Sheriff Jack Applebee stepped forward and handcuffed both men, Frangiamore's mother rushed to him. "My boy! Oh, my boy!" Frangiamore's mother cried out, clinging to her son's arm.

136

Reporters asked Frangiamore about the verdict and his thoughts.

Frangiamore hung his head. "It's tough," he responded, shaking his head as he shuffled along.

Palisano refused to comment after the verdict, and his once carefree attitude completely dissolved. After both men were led into the Erie County Jail, they were taken to the office of Warden Matthew Hess, where they were booked and frisked.

A reporter for the *Times* followed both men, witnessing what occurred next:

> *It was a pitiful sight as Frenchmore's* [Frangiamore's] *mother asked admittance to the office. Rules of the jail did not permit it, but Mr. Hess unfastened the handcuffs and Sam kissed his mother good bye, through the bars of the jail door. Tears streamed down his cheeks. He kissed her over and over again and then came his sister and two former pals. He shook hands with them and as he was locked up—cut off from the outside world until he finished his prison sentence, whatever it may be.*

As Frangiamore was led to his cell, the reporter followed, peppering him with questions.

"I can't say anything," Frangiamore responded, "The breaks were all against me. I'm going to do time for something someone else did."

As the turnkey unlocked the cell door, Frangiamore turned to Warden Hess. "All right for me to go in there, Mr. Hess?" Frangiamore asked politely

"Go right ahead. Your ticket's all paid for." Hess responded.

Judge Rossiter denied the motion for new trials for Frangiamore and Palisano on Monday, September 24, 1928, and immediately sentenced both men. Salvatore "Sam" Frangiamore was sentenced to serve ten to twenty years at the Western Penitentiary, and Anthony Palisano was sentenced to serve seven to fifteen years.

When Judge Rossiter asked Palisano if there was any reason why he should not be sentenced. Palisano shrugged his shoulders and simply said, "I'm not guilty."

While plans were made for both men to be delivered to the Western Penitentiary by Deputy Sheriff Jack Applebee later that week, Frangiamore and Palisano's attorneys planned to file their appeal to higher courts.

CAPODECINA

Following the holdup of September 2, 1927, the Erie County Electric Company started paying employees by check, eliminating any possibility that such a daring crime could ever be replicated.

In 1943, the Erie County Electric Company merged with the Pennsylvania Electric Company, then known by its current name, Penelec. The building and garage at the corner of French and East Twelfth Streets remained for some time and housed the *Erie Dispatch* newspaper; however, it was later demolished. A gas station currently sits on the corner of French and East Twelfth Streets.

Gus Driggs remained with the Erie County Electric Company following the payroll holdup. An avid sportsman, Driggs was instrumental in the formation of the Erie County Sportsman's League and later owned the Terminal Gas Station at the corner of West Sixth and Cranberry Streets. Gus Driggs died from a heart attack at his residence in 1948 at the age of sixty-one. Following his death, Driggs was forever memorialized in the Erie Field Trial Club's annual Gus Driggs Memorial Spring Open Field Trial.

Ray Pinney remained with the Erie County Electric Company when it merged with the Pennsylvania Electric Company and worked as a sales representative in the commercial department there until his retirement in 1971. He passed away in Franklin, Pennsylvania, in 1985 at the age of seventy-nine.

Anthony Palisano served his sentence at the Western State Penitentiary and was paroled in September 1935. Following his release, Palisano returned to Buffalo, New York, and from all accounts, appears to have steered clear of any further criminal activity. He remained in Buffalo, where he married and raised his children until 1967, when he and his wife moved to Dunedin, Florida, and owned the Pine Tree Farms Meat Market there.

Anthony Palisano died in March 1979 at the age of seventy-two.

After spending several years at the Western State Penitentiary, Salvatore Frangiamore retained three local attorneys in Pittsburgh as he prepared to ask the state pardon board for parole in 1932. Frangiamore applied for a pardon in August 1934, which was protested by then–Erie County district attorney Mortimer E. Graham. Frangiamore's request for a pardon would ultimately be denied.

Frangiamore again sought parole the following year, and this time, he was granted a pardon by the state parole board in December. He was released on December 24, 1935.

Frangiamore's freedom was short-lived, and in 1936, he was arrested in Fredonia, New York, as a suspicious person by officers there. While he was being transported to the police station, Frangiamore managed to seize one of the officer's service revolvers and fired off a shot. Frangiamore was later charged with assault in the first degree on a police officer and was convicted. On October 7, 1936, Frangiamore was sentenced to a prison term of ten to twenty years at Attica State Prison.

Following his parole from Attica State Prison in 1944, Frangiamore resided in New Jersey before returning to Buffalo in 1956. There, he became involved with the Laborers Local 210 and several construction sites connected to the mafia. By this time, Frangiamore was heavily involved in gambling rackets sponsored by Niagara Falls mob boss Stefano Maggadino.

In the 1970s, the FBI examined the hierarchy of the Buffalo crime family. Frangiamore was rumored to have been one of three individuals in charge of a "figurehead role" and screened the activities of the other two leaders. With numerous convictions against him and declining health, Frangiamore soon retired as boss of the Frangiamore-Todaro regime in 1984.

Salvatore "Sam" Frangiamore passed away from natural causes on November 28, 1999, at the age of ninety-four.

Daniel "Danny" Sansanese, the third suspected bandit involved in the payroll robbery, had pleaded guilty on September 30, 1927, to the robbery at the Dambach Drug Store and was sentenced to serve seven to fifteen years at Auburn Prison in Auburn, New York.

A present-day photograph showing the corner of East Twelfth and French Streets. *Author's collection.*

Danny Sansanese was paroled by November 1932. In 1935, Sansanese was again implicated in another robbery in Buffalo and convicted for first-degree robbery. Because Sansanese was a second-time offender, he was sentenced to a maximum term of thirty years at Attica State Prison.

Sansanese was paroled from Attica in December 1944, and after he returned to Buffalo, he continued to ascend the hierarchy of the city's criminal underworld, becoming involved in numerous burglaries, gambling rackets and a handful of unsolved gangland slayings. In 1972, Sansanese was listed by the FBI as being the number one capo of the Buffalo crime family and was one of the most feared members of the mafia there.

Around this time, Sansanese's health declined, and he died in Buffalo in 1975 at the age of sixty-seven.

As for what happened to the $15,103.62 stolen on that bitter September morning in 1927, it remains as much of a mystery today as it was ninety-six years ago.

6

ANGEL OF THE BAY

Mary Sobucki and Erie's Infamous Baby Harvesting Farms

Thirty-five-year-old Frank T. Schauble, a local photographer, shuffled along the east side of the Erie Dock, near Loesch's Wholesale Fish, on the afternoon of Wednesday, March 18, 1931. Earlier in the day, threatening clouds swayed over the choppy waters of Presque Isle Bay. Water sloshed against the dock walls as a slight breeze licked his hair.

In the distance, seagulls screamed en masse as they swooped down into the waters. Nearby, the large concrete grain elevators towered over the water like a behemoth.

Schauble froze as his eyes zeroed in on something floating in the water: a body.

Schauble ran for help and came across Ernest G. MacMurdy, an employee at a gas filling station near the dock, and told MacMurdy what he saw. MacMurdy returned with Schauble and saw to his horror that a body, appearing to be female, was face down in the water.

MacMurdy notified the United States Coast Guard.

Captain Richard Herline, the commander of coast guard cutter 121, arrived just east of the dock in seventeen feet of water. With the assistance of other men, the crew retrieved the body from the water. The body, that of a woman, was incredibly heavy. As the men crowded around the corpse on the deck of cutter 121, they realized why it ended up in the bay.

Clearly visible was a rope tethered around the woman's neck, a large iron weight secured and carefully wired underneath her arms. An eight-foot-long

A bird's-eye view showing the public dock. Mary Sobucki's body was found to the left, just off the end of the East Canal Basin. *From the Erie County Historical Society.*

section of chain had been secured to the body, likely attached to a weight in the water.

The United States Coast Guard held onto the body until police arrived.

First on scene was Assistant County Detective Harry Russell. Minutes later, Detective Sergeants William Donahue and Jack Applebee of the City of Erie Police Department also arrived and began assisting Russell in the investigation. Coroner Dan Hanley had been notified of the discovery and assisted in the removal of the body to Hamot Hospital, where it would undergo an autopsy.

Detectives stared at the bloated blond-haired body that was already in an advanced state of decomposition. Any initial belief that the woman had ended up in Presque Isle Bay by any other means than suicide was discounted when the men inspected the iron and weights that clung to her body.

After the body was taken to the morgue at Hamot Hospital, police began to search nearby for clues that could provide any indication about what occurred and how she ended up in the water.

Left: Detective Sergeant Jack Applebee of the City of Erie Police Department. *From the* Erie Daily Times.

Right: Detective Sergeant William J. Donahue. *Courtesy of the Donohue family.*

More importantly, they needed to identify the victim.

Donahue and Applebee interviewed workers and fishermen employed on the docks and fisheries who may have been witness to anything out of the ordinary that occurred in the past month. A watchman who patrolled the area after dark told detectives it was not uncommon for vehicles to use the blind end of the dock road after dark as a lovers' lane.

The detectives learned the road near Loesch's Wholesale Fish was unusually dark and quiet at night. Also partially obscured by three old, discarded boilers, the area was a perfectly isolated spot in which to dispose of a body. The area could be accessed by one road that then let out onto State Street.

At Hamot Hospital, in the morgue, Coroner Hanley assisted Doctor Ernest L. Armstrong, a pathologist, with the autopsy.

The woman was about five feet, six inches, tall; weighed between 130 and 150 pounds; and had bobbed blond-, possibly auburn-colored hair. Extensive decomposition rendered her facial features so distorted that Armstrong felt it would be nearly impossible for anyone to recognize her. She showed no marks that indicated an attack or assault had taken place; however, there were several marks about her head, initially believed to be bruising. Dr. Armstrong later concluded this was most likely discoloration from decomposition.

State Street, looking north, toward the public dock. *From the* Erie Daily Times.

Judging by the state of decomposition, Hanley and Armstrong felt the body had been in the water for about two or three weeks. Both men also discovered something more shocking: the woman was pregnant with a seven-month-old female fetus.

Located near the woman's lower abdomen, Dr. Armstrong noted her intestines were torn and clotted, leading him to believe that a hastily performed abortion possibly was the cause of death. Only afterward was she then discarded into the bay, already deceased.

Also noted by Dr. Armstrong was the fact that the woman was fully clothed. The *Erie Dispatch Herald* printed a description of the woman's clothing, hoping to assist in her identification:

> *She wore a dark blue coat with gray fur collar and cuffs, a blue serge belted dress, with fancy design, pink slip, blue bloomers, black shoes and stockings and dark galoshes with red soles. A cheap breast pin set with a green stone surrounded by smaller stones of varied hue, a string of cheap large pearls and a handkerchief of fancy design were found on the body.*

Erie County district attorney Otto Herbst, Assistant County Detective Russell and Detective Sergeants Donahue and Applebee later arrived at Hamot Hospital and conferred with Coroner Hanley and Dr. Armstrong and performed a closer inspection of the rope, iron and chains found on the body.

Dr. Armstrong felt that the rope was used to lower the body into the water in order to prevent a splash, which would have attracted unwanted attention. The body, he added, had been in the water for at least two weeks. The heavy weight found with the body weighed around seventeen pounds, and it was likely used with the wire tied underneath her arms to prevent the body from surfacing.

When District Attorney Herbst later returned to his office, he was greeted by a drove of reporters. Herbst briefly stopped and spoke, telling them the unidentified woman was deceased before she was placed in the water.

The cause of her death was possibly a failed abortion. "Dr. Armstrong said that there is absolutely no doubt but what the woman was dead before her body was placed in the water," Herbst said. "It is a plain case of murder, but we are up against a stone wall until the body is identified. Not a single clue to the identity of the woman has been found so far."

When asked what the first steps would be for the investigation, Herbst responded: "Our first step is to identify the woman. Through that we can obtain some clues. Right now everything hinges on the identification."

That evening, police provided descriptions of the unidentified woman and her clothing through local radio station WEDH. A detailed teletype was forwarded to every town, city and hamlet in Pennsylvania. At police headquarters, a thorough search was made of all missing persons reports for women within the city and county, covering the past several months.

Neither the public appeal with details of the victim nor the search of records provided any clues for detectives.

That night, a bitter air smothered the bayfront. Donahue and Applebee returned to the lonely, isolated spot where the body was recovered. The area was darker than they imagined, with sparse lighting, save for the twinkling assemblage of lights of the city behind them.

Both men knew it would be a difficult case.

Assistant County Detective Russell, speaking to a reporter for the *Erie Dispatch Herald*, felt another piece of iron, heavier than the one found with the body, had possibly broken free or torn lose, allowing the gases inside the body to bring the bloated corpse to the surface.

The following day, the three detectives planned to set out into Erie's criminal underworld, where abortions were known to take place, to interview those connected with similar crimes, hoping this would assist in their investigation.

This angle, however, was considered a long shot. Dr. Armstrong informed the detectives that he believed the operation had been performed by an inexperienced person, making them much more difficult to trace.

Little did the detectives know, it would not be much longer before they had some answers, leading them to one of the most sensational crimes in the city's history.

BEWARE THE SHEIK

Forty-five-year-old Victoria Sobucki; her husband, Vincent Sobucki Sr.; and their twenty-one-year-old son, Vincent Sobucki Jr., traveled into Erie on Thursday, March 19, 1930, to market produce from their family farm in McKean Township, south of the city. While they were selling some of their produce on East Seventh Street, a family member notified Vincent Sobucki and his son of the body found in Presque Isle Bay.

They felt the description matched Vincent's daughter, Mary Sobucki.

The Sobucki family shrugged off the suggestion. Mary, who was twenty-two years old, was married and alive—at least, that's what they believed. The last time her family saw her was December 27, 1930, when she told her parents she was traveling to Buffalo, New York, to marry the father of her unborn child, a man named Anthony Weiczorkowski, also known as Tony Dempsey.

After the Sobucki family arrived at the office of the *Erie Dispatch Herald*, they were given a description of the woman and her clothing. Victoria Sobucki listened patiently as her son translated the descriptions. Suddenly, she felt a lump in her throat when her son described the belt, which was similar to one she had made for her daughter, Mary.

Pleading for more information, the Sobuckis were directed to Hanley's Undertaking Parlor. They arrived there with a *Dispatch Herald* reporter around 6:00 p.m. Because of the body's advanced state of decomposition, Hanley forbade them from viewing it. Instead, Victoria was shown a breast pin that had been removed from the woman's clothing. She was also shown a set of imitation pearls that had been recovered from the swollen neck of the woman.

It was then that Victoria Sobucki broke down in tears and nearly collapsed.

The dead woman was her daughter, Mary Sobucki.

Victoria Sobucki told Coroner Hanley that the family was aware she was pregnant and had learned of it the previous August. When asked if Mary would have consented to an abortion, Victoria vehemently denied her daughter would undergo such an operation. Mary, her mother added, intended to give birth to her child.

Mary Sobucki. *From the* Erie Daily Times.

As for the child's father, Victoria Sobucki named Tony Wieczorkowski. Wieczorkowski, Victoria claimed, promised Mary that he would divorce his wife, whom he also had a child with, as soon as possible so they could get married.

Victoria Sobucki, sobbing and angry, shoved her finger at Coroner Hanley. "Arrest that man," howled the embittered mother in broken English, "and you will have the murderer of my little girl! Arrest Tony Wieczorkowski!"

The *Dispatch Herald* reporter who arrived at Hanley's Undertaking Parlor with the Sobucki family raced to a nearby phone and called Detective Sergeant Donahue, informing him of the identification.

Within a half hour of the identification of the body, Detective Sergeants Donahue and Applebee pulled up in front of 556 East Fourteenth Street, the home of Eva Wieczorkowski. Inside, detectives located twenty-nine-year-old Anthony Joseph Wieczorkowski. After he was briefly questioned by detectives, Wieczorkowski confirmed he had been living with his mother for the past six months and was separated from his wife.

Anthony Wieczorkowski was taken into custody and driven downtown for further questioning. A short time later, Anthony's twenty-year-old brother, Frank Wieczorkowski, was arrested as a material witness and also taken to downtown for questioning.

In the office of George Christoph, the captain of detectives for the City of Erie Police Department, Anthony Wieczorkowski was questioned by Christoph, District Attorney Otto Herbst, Coroner Dan Hanley and Detective Sergeants Applebee and Donahue. Later, Victoria Sobucki and her son were escorted into the office, positioned only feet from the man she believed murdered her daughter and unborn grandchild.

Victoria Sobucki told Christoph and Herbst about the relationship between Wieczorkowski and Mary. In May of the previous year, Mary left for Erie, where she worked in a store owned by Nick Muntean at 1014 Pennsylvania Avenue. Mary worked until she discovered she was pregnant around August and later quit her job to return to the Sobucki farm in McKean Township, where she lived until she was last seen by her family.

Wieczorkowski was the man she had seen three or four times when he visited her daughter at the family farm in McKean Township; she had also

Anthony and Frank Wieczorkowski shortly following their arrest. *From the* Erie Daily Times.

met his brother Frank. The last time she saw them was Christmas Eve 1930, Victoria Sobucki confirmed. Mary's brother Vincent confirmed this to police and described Wieczorkowski as "Mary's sheik."

Victoria Sobucki said Mary packed her belongings after dinner on December 27 and disappeared afterward. Three days later, Mary's parents received a letter postmarked from Erie. Mary wrote that she was on her way to Buffalo to wed Wieczorkowski.

Anthony Wieczorkowski withstood the constant barrage of questioning from Christoph and Herbst but maintained he knew nothing about Mary's disappearance and had not recently read the newspapers. Grabbing copies of the *Erie Daily Times* and *Erie Dispatch Herald*, Christoph tossed them onto the table in front of Wieczorkowski. "Well, do you know who that is?" Christoph asked, thumping his index finger on the newspapers.

"No." Wieczorkowski shrugged.

"Well," Christoph responded, standing up, "that's your Mary."

Wieczorkowski looked down at the newspapers, uninterested. "I don't know anything about it."

In the two hours that followed, Wieczorkowski admitted to being intimate with Mary Sobucki but said he was unaware she was pregnant. Wieczorkowski claimed Mary had been running around with other men, which was the reason they broke up. "We broke up, and I forgot all about Mary," Wieczorkowski said innocently.

When questioned, Frank Wieczorkowski was evasive and argumentative with Christoph and Herbst, which only cemented further suspicion on him and his brother. After a half hour, Frank Wieczorkowski started to change his story and admitted to being present on automobile rides with Anthony and Mary.

When asked about a letter his brother had received from Mary in December, Frank Wieczorkowski feigned ignorance, only to admit that he had driven his brother to the Sobucki farm in McKean after his brother received the letter. When they drove up to the farm, Anthony said he sent one of Mary's younger brothers into the house to bring her outside. When Mary came out, she told Anthony she had had a misunderstanding with her parents and that she was going to Buffalo.

Frank and Anthony Wieczorkowski claimed that this was the last time either of them saw Mary Sobucki alive.

As the Wieczorkowski brothers were being interrogated, their mother arrived at the front desk. Soon, she became hysterical and had to be removed to her home. Four hours later, it was decided the police would hold both brothers overnight. Both brothers were considered suspects in Mary Sobucki's death and disposal in Presque Isle Bay.

When questioned about the arrests, District Attorney Herbst said, "These brothers may be innocent of any connection with the case, but Frank, by his evasive manner, has laid himself and his brother open to suspicion."

George Mead, a reporter for the *Erie Daily Times*, traveled to McKean Township on the evening of March 19. After he arrived in the small borough, Mead reported of whispers spoken among the men and women of the town about the poor, blond, huskily built woman who was murdered.

The poor woman, in trouble, left her small family farm for the city. She then disappeared in December without a trace.

At the McKean Post Office, Mead asked a schoolteacher about Mary Sobucki and what she knew about her. The woman became alarmed and walked away hastily.

Mead inquired about the girl almost everywhere, and he soon learned that Mary Sobucki was not as well known in McKean as she was in the Polish neighborhoods of Erie.

Mead then became acquainted with two young boys who promised to take him to the Sobucki family farm.

Soon, Mead traversed "over mud-rutted roads, off the paved highway, [to] a dimly lighted one-room farm house, [which] blinked hazely from the top of the knoll."

Mead knocked at the front door of the home. A few seconds later, the door opened, and Mead was faced with a "tired-looking unshaved middle-aged man," Mary's father, Vincent Sobucki.

"Does Mary Sobucki live here?" Mead asked.

"She's dead!" Vincent Sobucki responded glumly.

After a brief discussion, Mead was allowed inside the home, illuminated with oil lamps that cast "weird shadows" about the inside the house. Nearby, some of Mary's younger siblings clung to their mother, Victoria. Mead curiously noted later the lack of emotion from Mary's parents and siblings.

Mead asked Victoria Sobucki about her daughter and the last time she saw her. "Mary, last December, she go with Tony Dempsey," she responded in broken English. "Children and me look out window and see him loving Mary."

"Mary wrote to us," Vincent Sobucki said, looking around the cluttered home by lamplight, searching for the postcard they had received from their daughter, but he was unable to locate it.

Mead learned Mary met Anthony Wieczorkowski at a skating rink in Erie. Mary's parents believed that when he got divorced, he was going to marry their daughter. Mary's parents gestured to a part of the one-room farmhouse they occupied, where they hoped to display their daughter's body—their lovely daughter who loved well but unwisely. "Maybe we'll let her be buried from the undertakers. We haven't much money," Mary's parents admitted.

Before leaving the Sobucki home, Mead asked the family about Mary was like.

Mary loved to dance, her parents said. She loved to roller skate and didn't care for life on the farm. The tone and emotion from Mary's parents led Mead to believe they felt it difficult to keep a young girl of her looks and temperament out there in the country. Maybe she was right, Mead wrote.

On Friday, March 20, 1931, Anthony Wieczorkowski was questioned in intervals throughout the day by police. Wieczorkowski continued to deny he was involved in Mary Sobucki's murder.

While Wieczorkowski was being questioned, Detective Sergeants Donahue and Applebee visited the Standard Stoker Works, where Wieczorkowski was employed as a crane operator. When Wieczorkowski learned Mary's body had been recovered, his coworkers noticed a "marked difference in his demeanor," to the extent that Wieczorkowski was unable to properly function and operate his crane.

Donahue and Applebee were also taken to the garage where Wieczorkowski worked. Almost immediately, they discovered an iron weight identical to the one found on Mary Sobucki's body. A length of chain, similar to the one used to weigh down Mary's body, was found by a heavy window in the rear of the garage. To detectives, it appeared another chain was missing. Finally, rolls of wire of identical to that found on Mary's body were found in the garage.

After Donahue and Applebee left Wieczorkowski's employer, they followed up on leads related to two galvanized iron snaps that were used to fasten the chain around Mary Sobucki's body. This information led detectives to a hardware store on Parade Street, where a clerk there told the detectives Wieczorkowski had purchased additional iron snaps and claimed he was going to use them for a dog chain.

Donahue and Applebee also later learned Wieczorkowski had approached two men in an unsuccessful attempt to convince them to flee Erie with him.

Evidence obtained by Donahue and Applebee was presented and turned over to George Christoph and District Attorney Herbst the following morning. Together, both men, assisted by District Attorney Graham; his assistant, John Ignasiak; County Detective John Coates; and a stenographer, planned for another round of interrogations, this time armed with more evidence.

After four hours of questioning on Saturday, March 21, 1931, Wieczorkowski finally broke. "It's all up," Wieczorkowski cooly mumbled. "I did it. A long time ago, I did it. I choked her out near where I worked on Gaskell Avenue. Then I thought of throwing her in the lake."

His words spewed from within. "I met Mary Sobucki at the skating rink on Twelfth and French Streets early in 1930 and went out with her frequently," Wieczorkowski freely admitted, acknowledging he and Mary were intimate frequently.

He said Mary informed him in September that she was pregnant. He said she also had been telling everyone, including her family and friends, that he was the father.

Showing no emotion, almost frozen to his chair, Wieczorkowski continued his confession:

> She [Mary] said I was the father of her expected baby, but I was not. That is why I killed her and put her body in the bay. On December 23, Mary wrote a letter to me....Frank, my brother, and myself went to her

home in McKean. I told her to come to Erie on the night of December 29t and met her at the skating rink. Before the meeting, I placed the iron weight, a chain and a rope in the auto. We drove out the Buffalo Road until we came to Gaskell Avenue. I turned down that road until we crossed the Nickel Plate tracks and then left. I stopped the car near the Standard Stoker Works. I drew out the rope and put it around her neck and choked her for about ten minutes. Then I drove down to the dock and threw her into the water. There was nobody around that night. It was too cold and snowing too hard.

Wieczorkowski repeated his statement as a court stenographer sat nearby, typing out the confession. After signing the confession, Anthony Wieczorkowski was removed from the police department while handcuffed to Detective Sergeants Donahue and Applebee. The rest of the parties present during Wieczorkowski's confession followed, traveling to the public dock.

Standing in the frigid March wind, Wieczorkowski reenacted how he removed Mary's body from his car and dumped it over the side of the dock

The road near Gaskell Avenue, where Anthony Wieczorkowski claimed he strangled Mary Sobucki. *Author's collection.*

A present-day view looking at the area where Mary Sobucki's body was recovered from Presque Isle Bay. *Author's collection.*

into the frigid water. Afterward, the men traveled on Gaskell Avenue, where Wieczorkowski claimed he strangled Mary in his vehicle.

After the visits to the crime scenes, information charging Anthony Wieczorkowski with the murder of Mary Sobucki was presented before Alderman Eugene Alberstadt. Later that afternoon, Wieczorkowski was arraigned before Alberstadt and pleaded not guilty. Frank Wieczorkowski was held without bond as a material witness, and both brothers were sent to the Erie County Jail.

That Sunday evening, two empty seats remained at the dinner table of the Wieczorkowski home when a reporter for the *Erie Daily Times* was invited inside. Eva Wieczorkowski motioned to the empty chairs. "Tony and Frank always sat there," Eva Wieczorkowski said between sobs.

The atmosphere in the Wieczorkowski home was tense as the reporter spoke to John Wieczorkowski and Anna Pietrowski, the older siblings of Anthony and Frank Wieczorkowski. Also present was Frank's sweetheart. Eva Wieczorkowski told the reporter she had visited her sons earlier that afternoon, the first time since their arrest, after an appointment was set up

Anthony Wieczorkowski in the custody of Patrolmen David Doyle and Jack Bolan after leaving his arraignment before Alderman Eugene Alberstadt. *From the* Erie Dispatch-Herald.

by Emmett C. Wilson, a local attorney who agreed to represent Anthony the day before.

When asked about the murder and her son's confession, Eva Wieczorkowski dismissed any thought that her dear Anthony could be responsible for the murder. "Tony's a good boy. He never hurt anyone."

The Wieczorkowski family admitted they knew Mary Sobucki, as did the neighborhood, which was predominantly made up of Polish immigrants and their families. "Sure, we knew her," John Wieczorkowski admitted. "She lied about Tony. She lied to everybody."

Frank Wieczorkowski's sweetheart, who refused to give her name, knew Mary Sobucki and had worked on her hair several months before. "She told my friend she'd get Tony, some day. I didn't like her."

When asked about Anthony's relationship with Mary Sobucki, the Wieczorkowski family admitted they knew nothing about the relationship and that it was a secret to them until it was reported in the newspapers. The reporter from the *Times* interestingly also found out that Anthony had applied to be police officer with the City of Erie Police Department. Had it not been for this trouble, they insisted, he possibly could have been employed with the department.

On March 23, 1931, Frank Wieczorkowski was released on $1,000 bond. At the same time, funeral services were held for Mary Sobucki at the Hanley-Schaller Mortuary at Thirteenth and Peach Streets. After a brief service, the remains of Mary Sobucki and her unborn child traveled to Sterrettania and were then interred at St. Xavier's Cemetery in McKean Township.

Because Anthony Wieczorkowski's confession indicated the murder had been planned since September 1930, after Mary told him he was the father of her unborn child, the circumstances warranted a charge of first-degree murder, which carried the death penalty, said District Attorney Herbst.

Herbst was also insistent on bringing the case before the May grand jury and announced he would oppose numerous postponements that would delay the trial. Wieczorkowski's attorney Emmett Wilson started to prepare for the possibility of an upcoming trial.

Hearing he would most likely be charged with first-degree murder, Wieczorkowski remained unfazed. "I talked too much, I guess." Wieczorkowski admitted.

After it was announced that plans had been made to seek a charge of first-degree murder against Anthony Wieczorkowski, his family retained William Carney to prepare his defense. An Erie native, Carney was a graduate of Allegheny College and received a law degree from the University of Pittsburgh Law School. Admitted to the Erie County Bar Association in 1924, Carney was one of the most respected defense attorneys in Erie.

With an extensive knowledge of the law, Carney always remained an advocate for being heard as an attorney. Carney would always claim "that a lawyer should be heard by the folks in the back row of the courtroom, because someday, they might need a lawyer, and they will more likely remember the lawyer who speaks up."

Emmett C. Wilson withdrew his representation of Wieczorkowski. Hounded by reporters, Wilson said he would have no involvement with the defense and would not comment any further.

As Anthony Wieczorkowski's preliminary hearing was scheduled for March 27, Carney declared he had insufficient time to review the facts of the case and prepare before the scheduled hearing. Carney later met with District Attorney Herbst, and after a brief consultation, Herbst agreed he would not oppose Carney's request for a continuance.

Despite Wieczorkowski's preliminary hearing being postponed until April 1, District Attorney Herbst still planned for a trial day within the upcoming May term of court.

On Wednesday, April 1, 1931, Anthony Wieczorkowski was escorted under heavy guard from his cell in the Erie County Jail and taken to Alderman Alberstadt's office for the preliminary hearing scheduled for 2:00 p.m.

Cramped inside the alderman's office were members of Anthony Wieczorkowski's family, those subpoenaed as witnesses for the state and the family of Mary Sobucki, leaving many attorneys and reporters barred from the hearing. Outside Alberstadt's office, the large crowd continued to grow as they waited for a chance to glimpse Wieczorkowski.

As William Carney entered the alderman's office, he told the reporters present that a strong battle would follow to save Wieczorkowski from the electric chair. District Attorney Otto Herbst and his assistant, Mortimer E. Graham, appeared on behalf of the commonwealth.

The first witnesses who provided testimony were Ernest MacMurdy and Richard Herline, who discussed the recovery of Mary Sobucki's body from Presque Isle Bay on March 18. Testimony from Dr. Armstrong followed, in

Lowered the Body Into the Lake.

Anthony Wieczorkowski lowers Mary Sobucki's body into Presque Isle Bay. This illustration appeared in newspapers across the country. *From the* San Francisco Chronicle.

which he recited details from the autopsy report, confirming Mary's body bore no signs of violence, including strangulation, and that when it was found, there was no water in the lungs.

Despite finding evidence of a ruptured blood vessel, Dr. Armstrong said the cause of the resulting hemorrhages presented problematic findings in determining a cause of death. The hemorrhages, Armstrong argued, could have also occurred before Mary's body was discarded in the water.

When Assistant Prosecutor Graham asked Dr. Armstrong to state his professional opinion as to Mary's cause of death, Carney objected and was overruled by Alberstadt. Dr. Armstrong admitted that he was not able to express an opinion due to the state of decomposition. "Then after your findings, you would not be able to say whether death was due to natural causes or otherwise?" Carney asked.

Dr. Armstrong repeated he was not able to confirm a definitive cause of death.

A good portion of the preliminary hearing consisted of Carney and Herbst arguing for and against the introduction of Anthony Wieczorkowski's confession into evidence, with Carney objecting on the grounds that the commonwealth had not proven Mary died from anything other than natural causes. Herbst disagreed with Carney's argument, pointing out the rope, chain and weights secured to Mary Sobucki's body, while referencing previous case law that supported the commonwealth's argument.

Alderman Alberstadt overruled Carney's objection and ordered Wieczorkowski's statement be recited and entered into the record.

For much of the hearing, Victoria Sobucki wept at the mention of her daughter's name. When called to testify, she confirmed that she identified the clothing found on Mary's body and saw Anthony Wieczorkowski when he visited her daughter at their farm. "The last time I saw Mary was a few days after Christmas," Victoria sobbed.

As for Anthony Wieczorkowski, he sat among his family. Sometimes, he appeared concerned, but at other times, he seemed disinterested. It was noted that when he was in the presence of several women acquaintances, Wieczorkowski flashed a smile and had a different carefree attitude.

Mary's thirteen-year-old brother, Frank Sobucki, testified to the events that occurred on December 23, when Anthony Wieczorkowski and his brother, Frank, visited the family farm. George Christoph testified about his involvement in the confession and to being present when Wieczorkowski admitted to killing Mary Sobucki.

Detective Sergeants Donahue and Applebee testified to accompanying Wieczorkowski in an automobile to the locations he mentioned in his confession, adding that he spoke freely about the murder the entire trip. Other witnesses called were Frank Schauble, Deputy Coroner William Schaller and Anna Porowsky, the owner of 648 East Fifteenth Street, where Mary Sobucki resided for several months in 1930.

When asked if he planned to have Mary Sobucki exhumed for an additional autopsy, District Attorney Herbst said, "Such a course would be of no avail."

Upon the conclusion of the hearing, Wieczorkowski was discharged as a material witness, and after reviewing the facts of the case regarding Anthony Wieczorkowski, the judge ordered him to be held for the May term of court without bail.

A few weeks later, rumors indicated a possibility that Carney would ask for an additional continuance, pushing the trial back to the September term. The rumors turned out to be true, as Carney confirmed he would ask for another continuance, claiming he still had insufficient time to mount a proper defense, due partially to his workload with other cases leaving little time for Wieczorkowski's case.

On Wednesday, April 29, 1931, Carney filed the petition asking for the trial to be postponed until September. "It will be of vital importance that the exact cause of death be accurately and satisfactorily established. We will produce medical and expert testimony to the effect that the girl died from causes for which Dempsey would not be criminally responsible," the petition read.

A hearing on the petition was scheduled for the following day at 10:00 a.m. before Judge William E. Hirt. Herbst vehemently opposed further postponements, claiming Carney had more than a month to prepare for the case, and there was no reason why a delay should be granted.

At the hearing, both Herbst and Carney presented their arguments. Judge Hirt also brought up the rumors of a petition being filed for an exhumation. Both men agreed no petition to request an exhumation of Mary Sobucki's remains would likely be presented, adding an additional autopsy would be meaningless.

Carney argued the commonwealth had not proved a crime had been committed. "The state's pathologist has stated that his examination did not warrant his expressing an official opinion as to cause of the girl's death. I have checked the girl's life just previous to her death and expect to produce medical and expert testimony that she died from causes other than those charged against Dempsey."

Herbst, brief in his response, said Carney had had since April 1 to prepare and that there was no reason why the case could not proceed to trial. "The commonwealth cannot be held responsible for outcome of the case if the trail is postponed until September," Herbst argued.

Judge Hirt said that while he believed the defense counsel had insufficient time to prepare—and despite being inclined to refuse a motion for continuance—he would still review and take it under advisement. Later that afternoon, Carney's motion for a continuance was denied, clearing the way for trial, and the battle for the life—or death of Anthony Wieczorkowski in the Erie County Courts began.

CORPUS DELICTI

Anthony Wieczorkowski, dressed in a blue serge suit and light blue tie, entered Courtroom H of the Erie County Courthouse on the morning of May 11, 1931. Seated at the table next to his attorney William Carney, Wieczorkowski spoke freely with his siblings and mother, who sat behind him in the spectators' section. The *Erie Daily Times* remarked that the courtroom, filled to capacity, also held "hundreds of Wieczorkowski's friends and neighbors."

Because of the overwhelming crowds clamoring for a seat to attend the trial, deputy sheriffs were stationed at all the entrances to prevent further admission.

Court opened at 11:00 a.m. before Judge William E. Hirt. After Wieczorkowski entered a plea of not guilty, jury selection continued throughout the morning, with at least sixteen potential jurors questioned but not seated when court adjourned for lunch around 1:00 p.m. Selecting the jury proved difficult for both sides due to "announced pre-formed opinions or possession of conscientious scruples in connection with the return of a death penalty if the evidence warranted it."

A full jury of nine men and three women was not empaneled until the following morning after the opening of court. Before opening statements,

ERIE, PA.   Court House.

1482

The Erie County Courthouse. *From the Erie County Historical Society.*

the trial was moved to the courtroom of Judge Hirt, which was considerably smaller, meaning only family members for Wieczorkowski and Sobucki, along with subpoenaed witnesses and court attachés, could be granted entrance.

Hundreds of wishful spectators who were refused admission congregated around the door of Judge Hirt's courtroom.

Beginning his opening statement, District Attorney Otto Herbst spoke of Mary Sobucki and how her life came to an end on that lonely road north of Buffalo Road and how Anthony Wieczorkowski confessed to strangling Mary to death and later disposing of her body. These events, Herbst promised, would match following testimony from witnesses called by the commonwealth.

Wieczorkowski remained unmoved by Herbst's opening statement.

Frank Schauble, who first spotted the body, was the first witness to testify that morning, followed by Captain Richard Herline of the United States Coast Guard, who helped recover Mary's body. Herline identified the weight, chains and wire, presented on a nearby table, as the objects that were on the body when it was recovered. Ernest MacMurdy followed, reciting testimony that he was summoned to the scene that afternoon by Schauble and helped alert the coast guard.

Considerable attention was paid to Dr. Ernest Armstrong, who recited his findings from the autopsy report. Victoria Sobucki, Mary's mother, testified in the early afternoon. Assisted by a Polish interpreter, Mary's mother told the jury that she last saw Mary alive when she left the house on December 27, intending to meet with Anthony Wieczorkowski. "Mary was a good girl," Victoria Sobucki said with little emotion. "I knew she was going to have a baby, but she had always been a good girl."

William Carney objected to Victoria Sobucki's testimony, claiming the defense believed Mary had not died until the December 29, not December 27.

What followed was a half hour of arguments between Otto Herbst and William Carney before the next witness testified.

Frank Sobucki, Mary's brother, testified that Anthony Wieczorkowski arrived at their home on December 23 and spoke to his sister. Another witness, Bertha Karotko, testified that she saw Mary Sobucki shortly before her murder and that Mary had informed her she was about to have a baby. When cross-examined by Carney, Karotko claimed Mary informed her she intended to go through with an abortion. Despite Karotko testifying that Mary named Wieczorkowski as the father of her unborn child, through rigorous cross-examination, she retracted a significant part of her testimony, admitting "she didn't know who the devil the father was."

Wieczorkowski chewed gum as he listened to the testimonies, appearing disinterested in the trial.

That afternoon, Assistant District Attorney Graham introduced Anthony Wieczorkowski's confession into evidence. Judge Hirt, sensing a long back-and-forth between both men, decided to dismiss the jury for the day. Graham and Carney argued for nearly two hours, with Graham arguing the confession presumed a murder had been committed and was established. Admitting the confession, Graham said, would remove any reasonable doubt that a crime had been committed.

Both sides completed their arguments just after 6:00 p.m. Judge Hirt ruled the confession would be allowed into evidence and that the commonwealth could proceed.

On May 13, 1931, Anthony Wieczorkowski's confession was entered into evidence and read out loud in court, lasting just over an hour. After the confession was recited, the commonwealth rested. Before William Carney had the opportunity to begin his opening statement, Judge Hirt announced that every effort would be made to wrap up the trial for the jury, and if necessary, a night session would undoubtedly occur.

Addressing the jury, William Carney gave the defense's argument that Mary Sobucki had died from natural causes, not at the hands of Anthony Wieczorkowski. This evidence, Carney claimed, would hinge heavily on medical testimony brought before the jury.

The first witness called was County Detective LeRoy Search, who was present when Anthony Wieczorkowski's confession was obtained. Carney brought up allegations that Wieczorkowski claimed he had been abused by police while in custody, something Search denied.

"Didn't you say to Dempsey when you went to the police station that morning," Carney asked approaching Search, "that, 'I see you're sweating, it must be pretty hot for you,' and that 'it'll be a damned sight hotter if you don't come across'?"

"I did not," Search said.

Search confirmed Wieczorkowski was questioned for roughly forty-five minutes before he confessed to killing Mary Sobucki. The confession, signed by Wieczorkowski, confirmed he had not been beaten, threatened or made promises in exchange for his confession.

"What did you make him put that in there for?" Carney asked.

"Well," Search responded curtly, "I've had enough experience with confessions to know that defense attorneys always try to claim that the defendant was beaten."

Captain of Detectives George Christoph testified next, denying that Frank and Anthony Wieczorkowski were deprived of food while in jail at police headquarters. Detective Sergeant William Donahue, who arrested Wieczorkowski, repeated similar testimony to that from the day before, when he was called as a witness by the district attorney.

Erie County detective LeRoy Search. *Author's collection.*

Following a recess for lunch, the trial resumed that afternoon with witnesses who told of Mary Sobucki's lifestyle before her death. Jean Nehr, who resided with Mary from July to November 1930, admitted frequent association with the murdered woman, confirming that the two had many dates after dancing and skating. Nehr claimed Mary confessed she was suffering from an incurable disease and had recently spent six months in a county clinic seeking treatment. Nehr was just one of many witnesses who would show the defense's strategy that Mary was afraid to give birth.

On May 14, 1931, the final day of the trial, court opened with testimony from four local physicians. The first, Dr. Elmer Hess, testified about his thoughts of the autopsy report and cause of death. "The most probable cause of death which covers this autopsy record is a hemorrhage due to an attempted illegal abortion," Dr. Hess said while thumbing through the report. "There is no indication that death was caused by strangling."

When asked why he felt there was no sign of strangulation, Hess insisted that if strangulation had occurred, he would have expected to see marks left behind on the neck tissue. If Mary was strangled, as Anthony Wieczorkowski claimed, there was also the possibility that Mary's hyoid bone in her neck would have been broken or fractured. A broken or fractured hyoid bone, Hess said, looking to the jury, was common in strangulation.

Hess comfortably declared that if Mary was in fact strangled, despite the extensive decomposition to her body, signs would have been present.

The three additional doctors who testified following Dr. Hess, Drs. Chester McCallum, T.M.M. Flynn and Felix S. Shubert, provided similar testimony, which corroborated Dr. Hess's thoughts on the autopsy report.

Following a recess for lunch around 1:00 p.m., Carney began his closing arguments, eloquently asking they give Wieczorkowski freedom. The evidence, Carney said, confirmed Wieczorkowski's innocence and proved Mary Sobucki had died from natural causes as a result of an attempted abortion. Carney attacked the confession, claiming it had been obtained through intimidation and by starving his client.

A reporter from the *Erie Daily Times* who was seated in the courtroom said Carney's closing arguments were "brilliant and convincing."

After Carney concluded, District Attorney Otto Herbst addressed the jury. He immediately attacked Carney's arguments, claiming they were weak attempts to defeat justice from being served. "You heard the confession," Herbst said, his voice raised as he paced before the jury. "Dempsey certainly didn't make up that comprehensive document out of his mind, despite what the defense, through its imposing array of doctors, would have you believe— that this girl died from the effects of her own operation."

Herbst turned to the defense table, glaring at Anthony Wieczorkowski. "If she died from the operation as claimed by the defense, do you think it would have been performed while she was fully clothed?" Herbst cried loudly, his fists wringing with emotion before he again connected his gaze with the jury.

An eerie stillness settled in the courtroom as Herbst looked around, asking the jury that Anthony Wieczorkowski be convicted of first-degree murder and that justice be served for Mary Sobucki and her unborn daughter. Before Herbst could finish, one of Wieczorkowski's sisters in the audience stood up. "Stop him!" she screamed, pointing at Herbst. "Stop him! Shut him up!"

Anthony Wieczorkowski attempted to aid his sister before being restrained by deputies. Voices shockingly murmured from those in the audience as Judge Hirt's voice thundered, calling for order in the court. Deputies immediately removed Wieczorkowski's sister from the courtroom.

Following a short recess, District Attorney Herbst completed his closing arguments, and Judge Hirt began his charge to the jury, finishing just before 4:30 p.m. The jury then filed out of the courtroom to deliberate. By 6:30 p.m., the jury had not reached a verdict and were taken to dinner, returning an hour later.

Nothing further was heard from the jury room until about 10:00 p.m., when the foreman informed Judge Hirt that the jurors had reached a moot question and wanted further instructions from the court. Judge Hirt arrived thirty minutes later, along with Herbst, Carney and others. Wieczorkowski, who was sound asleep in his cell, was awakened and brought to the courtroom.

When speaking to the jury, Judge Hirt was asked if Wieczorkowski could be convicted even though he had not committed the murder; instead, he would be considered an accessory to the fact. Judge Hirt advised the jurors he believed they were going beyond the bounds of their deliberations and asked that only the evidence and law be considered in arriving at their verdict. "There is only one question for you to decide," Judge Hirt told the jurors. "Did this defendant commit the murder?"

If Weiczorkowski had committed the murder, it was necessary to determine the degree of his guilt, Judge Hirt declared. Regarding the element of corpus delicti, a Latin phrase meaning the "body of the offense or crime," Judge Hirt felt "corpus delicti has been proven beyond a reasonable doubt."

Following Judge Hirt's instructions, the jury returned to deliberate on the third floor of the Erie County Courthouse.

Around 12:30 a.m., members of the jury announced they had reached a verdict. It was later agreed the verdict would not be read until the following morning at 10:00 a.m.

The daily crowd of morbidly curious spectators and reporters clung to the hallways leading to Judge Hirt's courtroom that morning as those allowed into the courtroom filed in. Judge Hirt entered and seated himself before the jury as they filed into the courtroom. Annette Young, the clerk of courts, accepted the envelope from the foreman of the jury, George Luce.

Judge Hirt opened the envelope and read the decision, his face becoming visibly pale. He looked to the jurors without hesitation. "This is the grossest miscarriage of justice that has occurred in Erie County in many days!" Judge Hirt bellowed with unconcealed rage. "It is difficult for me to conceive what sort of evidence you would require to convict a man of first-degree murder."

Judge Hirt reclined in his chair as he passed the envelope back to Young in disgust.

Young read the decision.

"We, the jury, find the defendant not guilty."

The verdict swept over the room like a tidal wave as attorneys rushed to William Carney to congratulate him. Wieczorkowski remained stunned in his seat until someone jubilantly shook him by the shoulders, telling him he was free. Anthony Wieczorkowski stood up and backed away from the table. Assistant attorney Mortimer E. Graham reached over, shaking hands with him.

"I have no hard feeling toward anyone," Wieczorkowski told Graham, who nodded before walking away.

Anthony Wieczorkowski turned to his mother, almost falling into her arms as he began to sob. Nearby stood Weiczorkowski's sister, who clutched Anthony's young son in her arms. They, too, embraced and kissed before leaving the courthouse together.

Judge William E. Hirt. *From the* Erie Daily Times.

Those crowded outside the courtroom looked on in astonishment as they spoke wildly about the developments. In a corner of the hall nearby stood Victoria Sobucki, who sobbed uncontrollably. "There is no justice in this county," Victoria Sobucki said, shaking her head. "This isn't right. Mary was a good girl, and now she is dead. Mr. Herbst must do something."

Victoria Sobucki left the courthouse and walked across the street to the police department, where she met with George Christoph, demanding something be done. Christoph apologetically informed her there was nothing that could be done. Wieczorkowski, he said, had been found not guilty by a jury of his peers in accordance with the law.

The case, Christoph said, was closed.

Detective Sergeants Jack Applebee and William Donohue were equally bitter about the outcome. "We might as well quit after this," Applebee said exasperatedly to reporters. "I'm wondering if there is such a thing as justice."

As pandemonium and scandal reigned in the streets, jurors from the trial were paid for their services in the basement of the county courthouse. Roland Snellgrove, one of the jurors, was approached by reporters as he left the courthouse.

Snellgrove defended Wieczorkowski's acquittal. "We couldn't do anything else but find him not guilty," Snellgrove told the reporter. "All we could decide was whether or not he had committed the murder, and under the evidence, we decided he had not. We were convinced that he had thrown the body into the lake, but that didn't mean that he had committed the murder."

Snellgrove explained that originally, the jury had voted 10 to 2 for acquittal, with Snellgrove voting to convict. It was only after receiving further instructions from the judge the night before that Snellgrove changed his vote for acquittal.

District Attorney Otto Herbst, absent from the courtroom when the verdict was read, was nowhere to be found.

When news of Wieczorkowski's acquittal spread, the public reacted in a mixture of both outrage and disappointment. Harriet Powell of Erie wrote the following in a letter to the editor of the *Erie Daily Times*:

The complete exoneration of the confessed murderer of Mary Sobuski [sic]
by the jury's verdict of not guilty, indicates that the oratory of his brilliant
attorney was more powerful than facts. It has been reported that counsel
for the defense implied during the trial that the confession was obtained by
unfair methods, though no testimony was produced to substantiate the claim.
Innuendo, apparently, is effective and legitimate in some cases.

Some of the rage expressed toward the jury members, like Caroline Schmelzer, consisted of threatening phone calls: "Some of them called my wife the most insulting names one can imagine for her action on the jury," said Edward Schmelzer, Caroline's husband. "Unless the true facts in this care are run down and my wife is convinced all has not been told, she'll be held up to public scorn, along with other jurors for years to come."

Edward Schmelzer pledged $500 toward a fund for retaining a private detective agency to investigate the death of Mary Sobucki. O. LeRoy Heaton, another member of the jury, pledged to donate to the fund.

While the jury felt Wieczorkowski was not guilty of murder, it was clear they felt he was not entirely absolved of involvement in the circumstances surrounding Mary's tragic death. The jury also felt that despite Wieczorkowski's confession, which they said was unconvincing and illogical, they felt he still likely held all the answers.

The *Erie Daily Times*, in its "Radio, Electric and Magazine" supplement, on May 16, 1931, took out a full-page article and, in large, bold letters, asked: "What Has Happened to Justice?"

The article, which discussed recent local miscarriages of justice, claimed, a "Phantom Army of Murdered Men and Women March Across Black Pages of Criminal History—Their Killings Unavenged!"

Following his silence after Anthony Wieczorkowski's acquittal, District Attorney Otto Herbst announced he was reopening the investigation into the murder of Mary Sobucki. Additionally, Detective Sergeants Jack Applebee and William Donahue were asked to investigate reports that supported Wieczorkowski's innocence.

Although the case was reopened, Herbst urged caution. "I am ready to act at once if we receive something definite to work on. I have heard many rumors and reports since Wieczorkowski was freed, but I cannot help but feel that if the jury could not accept the signed confession, nothing can be done with mere rumors."

While Wieczorkowski was acquitted of murder, District Attorney Herbst confirmed the possibility that he could face additional charges for the illegal disposition of a dead body. Herbst confirmed that the plans of jury members to hire a private detective agency would not materialize, as there was a question of the legality of such a fund.

Even as District Attorney Herbst reopened the investigation of the murder of Mary Sobucki, fallout against members of the jury continued. One member of the jury fled the city due to fear and criticism. Another became ill after being threatened.

Backlash from the public prompted jury foreman George Luce to write a letter to the editor of the *Erie Daily Times*, defending jury's actions: "I have served as juror many times and in my judgment the jurors on this case were the most capable I have ever known. If the people, who criticize this verdict, had served in our position, I believe the verdict could not have been different."

Luce also took aim at the public and their threats against members of the jury: "Could you, who have expressed your views so prominently, bear the burden as you have asked of us? Could you retire at night with such a conscience?"

The *Erie Daily Times* explored the possibility of matching funds raised by citizens to retain private investigators to find out who killed Mary Sobucki. Victoria Sobucki was also determined to see justice was served. On May 21, she and her son Vincent appeared at the district attorney's office.

Victoria Sobucki demanded to know what was being done to locate her daughter's murderer. "She died from an illegal operation, and Tony Wieczorkowski knows all about it," Victoria Sobucki said to Assistant County Detective Harry Russell. "Tony knows who performed the operation, and when he confessed, he was shielding someone."

In the days following the end of the trial, the City of Erie Police Department continued to receive information from the public in relation to the murder of Mary Sobucki. These reports, George Christoph later told a reporter, contended that Mary Sobucki's death was involved with a known local abortionist. "If any person knows the true facts in the case, it is their duty as a law-abiding citizen to report them to officials at police headquarters," Christoph said to reporters. "Any information will be kept in strict confidence, and the identity of the informant will not become known."

District Attorney Herbst's investigation focused on another dark, sordid avenue of the city's criminal underworld: Erie's infamous baby harvesting farms.

FARMS OF DEATH

When the United States went dry at midnight on January 17, 1920, it was the beginning of a surge in crime from the shores of Maine to the beaches of California. Nestled along the shores of Lake Erie, Erie was strategically surrounded by larger cities plagued with smuggled alcohol and surging crime, making Erie the midway point for those with wicked intentions.

One of the crimes that occurred in Erie that is rarely discussed was the historical practice of baby harvesting farms. Known in history as "child harvesting," the term *baby farm*, rooted in late Victorian Britain, derived from the practice of accepting custody of an infant or children in exchange for payment.

One of the most sensational cases to occur in Erie happened on April 7, 1921, when twenty-two-year-old Marjorie Freeman and Betty White, who claimed they were nurses, were arrested and charged with performing a criminal operation on Ruth Ramsay of Girard Township.

Ruth Ramsay, a woman of small build with a dark complexion and black hair, was hospitalized at Saint Vincent's Hospital. Detectives learned several days before that Ramsay, a telephone operator at the Reed House, was removed from her position there when she disclosed she was pregnant.

When her family was told of her delicate condition, she was ejected onto the streets. When detectives looked for the father of Ramsay's unborn child, they were told he had showered her with promises of marriage but then disappeared. Unable to locate him, Ramsay believed she was left with no other recourse than to have an abortion.

When Marjorie Freeman and Betty White were arrested, Dr. Maxwell Lick performed surgery on Ramsay, whose injuries as a result of the supposed attempted abortion by Freeman and White endangered her life. "I can say only this," Dr. Lick told reporters on April 7, "the girl is very seriously ill, and it is absolutely necessary that she should have an operation; otherwise, I cannot comment on the case."

Marjorie Freeman and Betty White were arraigned before Alderman Bassett and held on $1,000 bond.

Detectives learned Freeman and White were living on the second floor of 418 West Eighteenth Street and that it was known they performed illegal abortions there for an extended period, purchasing doctors' appliances disguised as nurses. Police also learned it was not uncommon to see young girls, between the ages of fourteen and twenty, coming to and from the residence during all hours of the night—but never during the day.

418 West Eighteenth Street. *Author's collection.*

The *Erie Daily Times* reported Freeman and White were able to procure almost any type of surgical instrument available to allow them to perform the abortions.

At the time of their arrest, Freeman and White had vacated 418 West Eighteenth Street and were getting settled at another location. Detectives confirmed a local doctor of "considerable prominence" was involved with the operations at 418 West Eighteenth Street and was known to have spent many hours visiting the home.

Whether the doctor carried out his trade with the women acting as nurses, detectives did not know, but they had evidence that Freeman and White had performed the attempted abortion on Ramsay themselves.

As police investigated further, a social worker called at the Crawford restaurant, on the ground floor of 418 West Eighteenth Street, trying to locate Freeman and White. The social worker informed the restaurant that a fourteen-year-old girl had given Freeman and White seventy-five dollars to perform an abortion but that the women had moved following the girl's visit with the money. The fourteen-year-old had chosen not to go through with the abortion, and the social worker was attempting to collect the money, which had been stolen from the girl's uncle, who was poor.

On the morning of April 8, a reporter for the *Erie Daily Times* provided an astonishing story on the horrors that occurred at 418 West Eighteenth Street:

This illegitimate child was brought to the home of the two alleged "nurses" at 418 West Eighteenth street not more than three months ago....The mother of the child was but 18 years old and lived with her parents in this city. When the child was brought to the "nurses" home it was wrapped in medicated cotton. A well-known physician, who was in no way implicated in the work, was called, and he said that the child had been prematurely born on account of the criminal operation and could not live....When the child died I was called by Miss Freeman and she asked me what to do. I told her to have the child properly buried, and she called a prominent Erie undertaker. He demanded the name of the parents before he would bury the child, but the "nurse" told him she couldn't tell him, as she didn't know their names....I think the "nurse" obtained the names of the parents as the child was buried the next day. The "nurse" was given permission to attend the funeral. The child was buried in Lakeside cemetery. The casket was ordered and paid for by the "nurse," who told me on frequent occasions that she received from $200 to $500 every time she performed an operation....I have also been in the home for the "nurses" when young girls would come there. They ranged in age from 14 to 20 years. As soon as an operation was performed the girl would be sent home immediately unless she was in a weakened condition. There was a hospital bed in one of the rooms where a girl would be allowed to lay if she was weak after the operation.... Miss White's home is in Avonia, located near Fairview. She lived with her grandparents who have requested her time after time to come home and live with them, but she refused....She is but eighteen years old and after Miss Freeman was arrested several months ago, passed as her daughter. Miss Freeman gave her a beating one night and was arrested. She told police that she was the mother of Miss White and was not fined....Miss White was given very little of the money received from the criminal operations and was often without money. When Miss Freeman would go away she would be forced to borrow money in order to purchase groceries....Miss Freeman is twenty-three years old and told me that she was married when eighteen years of age. She also said she had a boy five years old who lives in California, where she claims her parents, who are wealthy, reside. I later learned that Miss Freeman's parents lived in or near Union City where her father was a laborer on the railroad.

Plumbers were also given $150 to not report what was found in the sewer during one incident. The job was completed by a prominent plumbing company, which worked all night.

The *Times* continued

> *The plumbers were called one afternoon when the sewer was not in working order. They worked all that afternoon, the following night and the next afternoon until 3 o'clock. When they found what was the cause of the sewer being out of order they began talking….The "nurse" then gave them $150 if he would say nothing about what was found in the sewer….I was told by the "nurse" that the plumbers had discovered an embryo child in the sewer and that in order not to have them say anything she gave them $150. I know the name of the plumbing firm, as do several other parties, but I would rather not tell it for the publication.*

Reporters speculated that doctors connected to operations at 418 West Eighteenth Street could face charges, even arrest, for their roles in the abortion scheme. Rumors flew wild that these secrets and more could be revealed during the upcoming May term of court.

On April 8, 1921, Marjorie Freeman and Betty White were released on $1,000 bond each. Newspapers claimed the funds for White's release were provided by a relative, and Freeman's were provided by "friends."

Rumors suggested the bonds were furnished not by friends but by several prominent Erie doctors connected to operations conducted by Freeman and White. Alderman Bassett refused to reveal the names of the individuals to the public. "The people who signed the bonds asked me to keep their names out of the press, owing to their business connections. It is customary to keep the names of people who go on bonds out of the press."

As Marjorie Freeman and Betty White remained free on bail, Ruth Ramsay remained confined to her hospital bed following her surgical procedure at Saint Vincent's Hospital. Doctors regarded the surgery as a success and gave Ramsay a good chance of recovery, despite her condition remaining the same and not entirely without danger.

As the district attorney's office prepared for a preliminary hearing, Ruth Ramsay's family obtained the services of an attorney to look after her interests.

Detectives learned of a piece of paper Ruth Ramsay had turned over to her relatives and friends in the event she did not to survive her injuries. The piece of paper had Marjorie Freeman's information, including her address and phone number, and it was given to her by her doctor A.H. Ireland.

The preliminary hearing for Marjorie Freeman and Betty White opened on April 16, 1921, before Alderman Bassett. Ruth Ramsay was the only witness called and testified, and she was sent to Marjorie Freeman and Betty White under the direction of her doctor. Prior to arriving at 418 West Eighteenth Street, Ramsay admitted she had used an instrument on herself and attempted to induce an abortion.

The case against Marjorie Freeman and Betty White was discharged by the May grand jury, which found insufficient probable cause that a crime had been committed.

Marjorie Freeman and Betty White were free.

Erie's connection to baby harvesting farms did not end there. In May 1925, Erie was further linked to a baby harvesting farm in New York, in which twenty-two infants died. In August 1929, Elizabeth Selsle, the head of the Union City Hospital, was arrested on charges that she performed an abortion which caused the death of a woman named Caroline Braden.

When the body of Mary Sobucki was found in Presque Isle Bay in March 1931, baby farms were still operating within the city of Erie and as far away as Union City, despite herculean efforts of law enforcement to eradicate their presence.

Details of Herbst's investigation into Mary Sobucki's death and the connection to baby harvesting farms vanished from the local press following the sensational trial of Anthony Wieczorkowski—until 1935.

Mortimer E. Graham, the assistant district attorney under Otto Herbst in 1931, was now district attorney for Erie County. For months, Graham's office received numerous complaints that a baby farm had been flourishing near Erie, and on Tuesday, January 29, 1935, both state and county authorities opened an investigation.

The proprietor of the baby farm, an older woman, was known to local authorities. Young girls from Erie and the surrounding territory had been seen frequenting the area. This was confirmed by individuals who performed deliveries to the house and become suspicious after seeing many young girls on the premises.

Informants also claimed the female proprietor of the baby farm used no instruments and that the fetuses were disposed of using incineration, which took place on the property. Because authorities deemed the complaints as credible, the *Erie Daily Times* predicted an arrest would soon occur.

Graham's office also obtained a statement from Frances Padavoni, who was hospitalized at Saint Vincent Hospital after having an abortion performed at the property. She feared that she was dying. Padavoni told police she was taken to the home on the night of January 24 and returned two more times between January 28 and January 31.

On January 31, between 6:30 p.m. and 7:00 p.m., Padavoni said she delivered the fetus, which was then fed to a pack of rabid dogs.

The remainder of Padavoni's statement was so grotesque and horrific that the *Erie Daily Times* and *Erie Dispatch Herald* were unable to print it. After she became ill on February 3, Padavoni called a physician, who kept watch over her for twenty-four hours. When her health deteriorated, she was admitted to the hospital.

On Monday, February 4, 1935, several Pennsylvania state cruisers, assisted by County Detective Leroy Search and led by District Attorney Graham, descended on 423 Laird Avenue, just south of Trinity Cemetery. State troopers exited their vehicles, stepped into the slushy street and made their way to the home, which was surrounded by an iron-spiked fence, with guns drawn.

State troopers grappled with several dogs on the property as Graham made his way to the front porch, where he pounded his fist against the front door. Soon, seventy-seven-year-old Minnie Falkenstein stepped out of the home in handcuffs. Also arrested was thirty-five-year-old Dominic Padavoni, the husband of Frances Padavoni.

A score of state troopers searched the home and property for the furnace that was rumored to have been used to incinerate the corpses of fetuses. The *Erie Daily Times* said the raid was the first enacted upon several known baby farms operating in the city, with anonymous sources telling reporters: "The present drive will not cease until all have been eliminated."

Later that day, Dominic Padavoni was released after questioning, in which he denied taking his wife to Minnie Falkenstein's residence. Padavoni also denied rumors that he had paid Falkenstein to perform the procedure. After visiting the farm, state police investigators heard that some of the contents taken from the dogs' internal organs could have been discarded fetuses, but they were unsure. "It's just hearsay so far as we're concerned," one trooper told a reporter.

Downtown, when questioned by police, Minnie Falkenstein defiantly refused to answer questions as she chewed on a large cigar protruding from her mouth.

The next day, Minnie Falkenstein was arraigned before Justice of the Peace Walter Goodwin. She pleaded not guilty to charges of performing an abortion and performing an abortion which resulted in death. After Minnie furnished bail in the amount of $2,000, provided by her third husband,

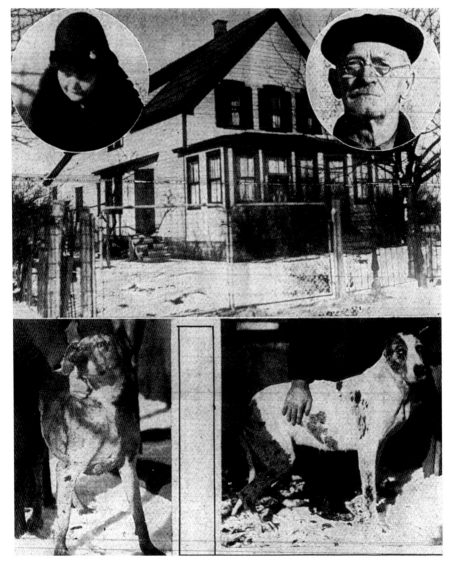

423 Laird Avenue. Minnie Falkenstein and her husband, Godfrey, are pictured, as are two of the dogs that were found on the property. *From the* Erie Daily Times.

Godfrey Falkenstein, a preliminary hearing was set for Friday, February 15, 1935, at 2:00 p.m.

As Falkenstein exited Goodwin's office, she walked through a group of reporters who pummeled her with questions about the arrest and the baby farm operation. "See my lawyer," Falkenstein replied calmly.

Further searches of Falkenstein's property failed to reveal surgical instruments that could have been used in any abortion procedure. Falkenstein's husband, whom police believed was innocent of any wrongdoing, said he knew nothing of Minnie's activities, although he did confirm strangers were around the house at various times.

When asked about the dogs, Godfrey Falkenstein pleaded ignorance, claiming he knew nothing about them. Minnie was responsible for the dogs, he claimed.

For those in Erie who could remember, including seasoned detectives, Minnie Falkenstein was well acquainted with trouble in Erie.

In October 1905, a gentleman by the name of Henry Froess secured the services of Minnie, whose surname was then Salow-Joachim, to perform an abortion on a woman named Sylvia Ruess. Ultimately, the abortion resulted in the death of Reuss's infant.

The following month, Minnie Salow-Joachim became the first woman tried in Erie County on a charge of willfully taking human life. She was later found guilty of voluntary manslaughter and sentenced to nine years in the Western Penitentiary.

By 1914, Minnie had been released from prison and married Godfrey Falkenstein. The two of them then resided at 423 Laird Avenue, where it was said she continued the practice of baby harvesting uninterrupted until 1935.

As quick as it had begun, however, the case against Minnie Falkenstein began to crumble when Frances Padavoni recanted her original statement on the afternoon of Thursday, February 21, 1935, when all parties appeared before Justice of the Peace Walter E. Goodwin.

The only witness called by Assistant District Attorney Illig, Padavoni denied not only the contents within the statement but also its implications and said that when she was hospitalized in Saint Vincent, she was too ill to know what she was saying. Following Padavoni's testimony, there was no further cross-examination, and Falkenstein was released with the charges against her dismissed.

Minnie Falkenstein saw District Attorney Graham's grand plan to end all baby harvesting farms in Erie County come to a sudden halt.

Did Minnie Falkenstein really feed the discarded corpses of fetuses and infants to dogs? Did she truly incinerate them on her property? State police investigators never conclusively confirmed this, and the searches on her property yielded no such evidence to support these accusations; however, those files have never been released to the public.

SECRETS FOREVER CONDEMNED TO THE GRAVE

After his acquittal, and with rumors of additional charges against him being presented, Anthony Wieczorkowski, his wife and their son fled the city on May 17, 1931, to an undisclosed location.

Wieczorkowski's marriage never recovered. His wife filed for divorce on November 30, 1932, claiming cruel and barbarous treatment in addition to Anthony's alcoholism, which increased in severity over time. He also reportedly beat and choked her and threatened to kill her and set the house on fire on numerous occasions.

The divorce was finalized on December 1, 1932.

The day after his divorce, Anthony Wieczorkowski married twenty-eight-year-old Helen Borchick of Erie in Westfield, New York, and left for Buffalo, New York, where they spent their honeymoon with one of Anthony's sisters, who lived there.

Anthony Wieczorkowski's second marriage soon deteriorated, and afterward, his criminal past returned.

On October 2, 1933, Anthony Wieczorkowski and his brother Frank were arraigned and charged with drunkenness and disorderly conduct. Both were arrested the night before, when Frank threatened to shoot members of a local gang who were threatening him and Anthony. When one of the brothers was attacked, Frank and Anthony engaged in a brawl. Anthony was struck in the jaw, and Frank, armed with a shotgun and blackjack, attempted to corral the gang members and take them to police headquarters.

Both brothers refused to press charges, and two of the opposing gang members were released. Frank and Anthony Wieczorkowski were each fined five dollars by Alderman Frank Gaczkowski and released.

A little over two weeks later, on October 17, Anthony and his brother John were arrested in the early morning hours after their car jumped the curb and went through an iron fence in front of a home on East Tenth Street. Both men were held without charges pending a warrant.

Anthony Wieczorkowski found himself in trouble with the law, along with his brothers John and Frank, when the three men engaged in a fight with their brother-in-law Joseph Pietrowski at a club on Thirteenth Street between Reed and Wayne Streets in February 1934. Pietrowski filed charges claiming the men had assaulted and threatened him. Four of the men, including Pietrowski, were later released after paying costs.

Anthony Wieczorkowski's name disappears from most records after the 1950s, when he was last known to have been living in Erie.

His whereabouts currently remain unknown.

Frank Wieczorkowski, arrested as a material witness in the investigation against his brother for Mary Sobucki's death, was shot and killed by a policeman on July 30, 1936. Wieczorkowski, brandishing a .38-caliber revolver, attempted to hold up a man while he was parking his automobile in a garage on East Ninth Street after chasing a woman who had run into the garage for protection.

Police were notified, and soon, Patrolman Patrick McDannel came face to face with Wieczorkowski in the rear of 150 East Ninth Street. When Wieczorkowski refused to drop his gun, McDannel fired a shot from his revolver. The bullet struck Wieczorkowski on his left side.

After being rushed to Hamot Hospital, Wieczorkowski died from his wounds that morning.

Otto Herbst refused to seek another term as district attorney and later returned to private practice in Erie, working alongside Samuel Y. Rossiter. Active in local Republican political circles, Herbst quietly lived the rest of his life out of the spotlight, choosing instead to remain an ardent reader of all forms of literature. He was known as one of the best-informed locals on current events in the world.

Despite enjoying his tenure as a prosecutor, Herbst always said he would have enjoyed the life of a newspaper reporter had he been given another chance

Herbst suffered a sudden heart attack at his home on August 11, 1939, at the age of fifty-two.

William Carney later served as district solicitor for the Erie City School District until 1970. During World War II, he served in Alaska and the Aleutian Islands as a judge advocate in the U.S. Army, and he held the rank of lieutenant colonel.

In 1953, Carney operated his law office, Carney and Carney, alongside his younger brother Edward; the firm was located in the Masonic building at Eighth and Peach Streets. After Edward was elected judge, William Carney eventually moved to 254 West Sixth Street with attorneys Mike Palmisano and Joe Walsh, where they worked alongside Wendell Good, Dick Brabender, Kim Moffatt, Richard Cowell, Jack Wingerter and Lee Fuller, establishing the law firm Carney and Good.

William Carney passed away at the age of seventy-three on October 2, 1972, from heart failure.

Leroy Search remained a county detective until 1944, when he took over as temporary head of the Erie County Probation Department, a position he was permanently appointed to in 1946. He remained in charge of the department until he passed away in 1948 at the age of fifty-seven.

Detective Sergeant Jack Applebee later became a candidate for county sheriff but was defeated in the general election. He remained with the Erie City Police Department until his death in 1937 from a heart attack at the age of fifty.

William Donahue served as a detective sergeant with the City of Erie Police Department until 1943, when he was promoted to the rank of captain. On November 1, 1946, he was promoted to the position of chief of police under the administration of Mayor Charles Barber, a position he held until 1947, when he retired after serving for forty-six years. When he was interviewed by a reporter from the *Times* in his family home in the first ward, Donahue reminisced, "All I ever want to be remembered as is a damn good copper."

Donahue passed away on June 2, 1968, at the age of eighty-two.

Victoria Sobucki spent the rest of her life believing the key to the murder of her daughter and grandchild rested with Anthony Wieczorkowski. In 1962, she celebrated her fifty-fifth wedding anniversary with her husband. She passed away the following year at the age of seventy-seven. Her husband, Vincent Sobucki, continued tending to the family farm in McKean until his death in 1966 at the age of eighty-nine.

Mary Sobucki's parents never learned the truth about who murdered their daughter and unborn grandchild.

The horrific murders of Mary Sobucki and her unborn child were never positively connected to Minnie Falkenstein or any of the other known baby harvesting farms in Erie. Details of the Erie County district attorney's investigation into the search for Mary Sobucki's killer, which was reopened after Anthony Wieczorkowski's acquittal, remains unknown to this day, with the records possibly long lost or destroyed.

Minnie Falkenstein's run-ins with the law continued after 1935. Forever suspected of involvement in abortion mills, Falkenstein was again the subject of an investigation in 1946, when police located a one-and-a-half-year-old child, known only as Nancy, in the home at 423 Laird Avenue living in deplorable conditions.

When asked by police about Nancy's parents, Falkenstein claimed the child had been given to her after she was born in her home. When pressed for additional information, Falkenstein refused to reveal the name of the parents.

On Tuesday, June 11, 1946, Deputy Sheriff Harold Tompkins took custody of Nancy and was told to appear in court by noon. Minnie Falkenstein was

The grave of Mary Sobucki in St. Francis Xavier Cemetery. *Author's collection.*

informed that if she appeared, she would need to give reasons why the small child should not be taken from her custody.

Falkenstein failed to appear.

Nancy was later sent to the Erie Infants' Home, and the case against Falkenstein was abruptly closed. Minnie Falkenstein died several years later at the age of eighty-seven on September 11, 1951.

Today, Mary Sobucki's murder officially remains unsolved.

Despite the case slipping into obscurity following Anthony Wieczorkowski's acquittal, it gained national attention when an article appeared in the March 1932 issue of the *Illustrated Detective Magazine*, titled "Non-Payment." The article was written by *Erie Daily Times* reporter Clifford Webb, who penned most of the *Times*'s articles on the case in 1931.

Webb's article ended with the following questions: "Do you think that this young and beautiful girl, with everything to live for, took her own life, or was the victim of some strange and accidental end? Do you think that the circumstances of this little drama of love and death failed to point out clearly the guilt of the man who freely confessed having perpetrated it?"

Those questions are still unanswered, as the remains of Mary Sobucki and her unborn child lay in permanent repose on the grounds of a small cemetery in McKean Township, the identity of those responsible known only to God.

7

SIN AGAINST THE LAW OF GOD

The 1936 Scarlet Sin Murders

*W*hen asked about the worst mass murder event that has ever occurred in Erie's history, locals will likely tell you about how thirty-eight-year-old Donald Chism murdered his estranged wife, their three children and their adoptive grandfather on the morning of January 27, 1975.

Found guilty and sentenced to five consecutive life terms, Chism was sent to prison, where he would later succumb to a heart attack. What those in Erie are unable to recall is the first sensational mass murder that occurred in the city thirty-nine years before.

And it began on a warm summer morning in 1936.

July 18, 1936, began as a perfect summer day in Erie, Pennsylvania. The sky was almost cloudless, and the sun glimmered brightly on the city, with scant humidity. The beaches of Presque Isle were sure to be visited by hundreds of families, and the neighborhoods were full of children playing in the streets and backyards.

It was just after 7:30 a.m. when Edna Reck stood on the front porch of her home at 2001 East Twentieth Street. Suddenly, Samuel Weed, a neighbor from across the street at 2114 East Twentieth Street, sprang from his home, clad in only a pair of shoes and trousers.

Weed, wild-eyed and on the verge of hyperventilating, stumbled to Reck's porch. "I killed them!" Weed sputtered, sobbing as he wiped drool from his mouth.

"You killed who?" Reck asked alertly.

2114 East Twentieth Street. *From the* Erie Dispatch-Herald.

"Irene and the babies!" Weed cried before darting off in the direction of Buffalo Road.

Reck immediately called out to her sons, Ralph and Richard, who were asleep in the backyard.

Ralph and Richard Reck then summoned a neighbor, Bert Strang, and the three cautiously approached the Weed home. Within a few minutes, the trio fled from the house in terror, informing Edna Reck that a gruesome sight awaited those who entered.

Irene Weed and her sons, Charles and David, had been murdered.

Edna Reck rushed to a telephone and called the police.

Two reporters from the *Erie Daily Times*, Ralph "Bat" Humble and Eugene Jana, arrived at the scene first. When they entered the bedroom where Irene Weed lay next to her son David, both men later recalled seeing a scene of absolute horror.

Both Irene and David Weed were unrecognizable, their features turned to a pulp of blood, flesh and bone. Irene Weed's head had been completely crushed in as she lay partly on her side, covered with a quilt. David's head, nestled against her arm, was crushed in. Next to him lay a bloodstained child's storybook.

Left: Charles and David Weed. *From the* Erie Dispatch-Herald.

Right: Irene Weed. *From the* Erie Daily Times.

A hammer, covered in blood, hair and brain matter, lay next to Irene Weed's body.

The reporters' attention was directed to the corner of the room, toward a crib. Both men tiptoed forward, looking inside the crib, which was also splattered with blood. Inside was three-year-old Charles Weed. His head, too, had been caved in. Both men were shocked when they noticed that Charles, although unconscious, was still alive.

Humble and Jana had decided they would try to get three-year-old Charles to a hospital immediately. As they were preparing to remove him from the crib, Officer Joseph Matlock pulled up in his cruiser in front of the Weed home.

Matlock was met by Humble and Jana, who were frantically telling him that two persons were dead, but one was still alive. Within seconds, the three men lifted the battered body of Charles Weed from his crib. They then bundled him into a blanket and jumped into Matlock's cruiser, en route to St. Vincent's Hospital.

While Officer Matlock and the *Times* reporters were in a desperate race to save Charles Weed, Samuel Weed was ambling along Buffalo Road. On one occasion, Weed attempted to throw himself under an approaching truck, but the driver managed to swerve just in time.

Lifting himself off the pavement, Weed deliriously stumbled into a nearby field, where he was spotted by Erie City police officer Carl Malinowski, en route to the Weed home.

Weed suddenly pranced from the curb near the corner of Buffalo Road and Wagner Avenue into the path of a vehicle that was heading west, driven by twenty-seven-year-old Glenn Hall of Wesleyville. Weed's head rammed into the fender of Hall's automobile, and he was hurled through the air after crashing through the passenger-side front window.

Weed's body landed several feet away, slamming against the ground.

Stumbling to his feet, Weed began bleeding profusely from severe lacerations on his scalp.

Malinowski screeched to a halt and darted from his vehicle in pursuit of Weed, who attempted to run. Malinowski managed to wrap his arms around Weed and tackle him to the ground.

"You're going to jail!" Malinowski yelled as he held Weed on the ground, attempting to handcuff him.

"That's alright," Weed exhaled. "I just got done killing my family."

Malinowski lifted Weed from the ground and walked him to his cruiser, where he placed him into the back seat. From there, Weed was transported to police headquarters and booked on an open charge before he was removed to Hamot Hospital under heavy police guard.

At Saint Vincent's, the doctors were advised by Assistant District Attorney Burton R. Laub to waive all legal technicalities and rush Charles Weed into surgery to save his life. This was due to the fact that in 1936, it was against the law to operate on a child without permission from their parents, guardians or relatives.

Laub took responsibility for allowing the surgery to proceed while he tracked down a relative for permission. He later obtained verbal permission from Charles's grandmother Alice Chapin.

Doctors quickly rushed Charles Weed into surgery, where he was placed under anesthesia as doctors attempted to relieve pressure from his skull. His wounds, however, were too extensive, and he succumbed to his injuries at 12:55 p.m.

When Erie County Detective Leroy Search and District Attorney Mortimer Graham arrived at the scene, it was chaotic, with the road in front of the home clogged with vehicles and curious onlookers. Upon entering the home, Graham was visibly shaken. "Horrible," Graham murmured.

Surveying the scene, reporters glanced into the backyard, which comprised a detached garage and a playground. Children's toys were discarded around the yard, never to be played with again.

Meanwhile, police searched the house for additional clues. A castoff pattern of blood stained the ceiling of the bedroom, and bloody water was found in the toilet bowl, indicating Weed had cleaned his hands following the murder. Rummaging through the family's belongings, police also found several life insurance policies, many of them in the name of Irene Weed.

Aside from the few signs that indicated a murder had taken place, the one-story home was well furnished and very neat.

When questioned by police, neighbors confirmed seeing Weed the previous night when he traveled to a nearby grocery store. Neighbors remarked that on the previous Sunday, July 12, he had almost collapsed from heat exhaustion when playing with his sons and had to be assisted inside by his brother.

Following this incident, Samuel Weed returned to his job at General Electric. Coworkers told police that Weed appeared disconnected, his demeanor changed. He would not speak to some of the other men and appeared nervous and moody. Weed also appeared to make suicidal remarks, which his coworkers ignored at the time.

Since the accident on July 12, neighbors noted Weed's odd demeanor continued and said he seemed ill. Others noted his physical appearance, saying he was "getting awfully thin lately."

When he arrived at Hamot Hospital, Samuel Weed was attended by attending surgeon J.T. Strimple and interns Glenn J. Greer and Alan F. McGill. His lacerations were stitched and cleaned, although doctors remarked his brush burns were dirty, rendering a "thorough cleansing impossible."

When taken away for X-rays, Weed continued to announce his plans to end his life, telling Patrolman Andrew Vamos, "I'm going to kill myself, as I want to join my wife and children."

Weed was later removed to a room next to the men's surgical ward. Weak from blood loss, he remained motionless, his head heavily bandaged. District Attorney Mortimer E. Graham, Assistant District Attorney Burton R. Laub and Chief of Police George J. Christoph arrived in Weed's room, joined by reporters from the *Erie Dispatch Herald* and the *Erie Daily Times*.

Weed mumbled a confession, devoid of emotion:

> *I didn't want my wife and children to live, because they were white and clean, because I have committed a "cardinal sin"—no, a "scarlet sin.".. .I*

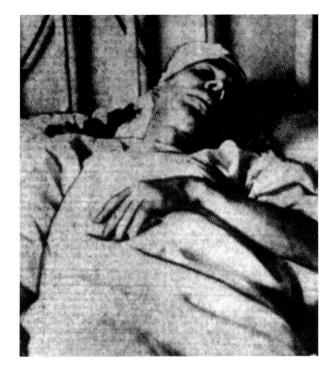

A hospitalized Samuel Weed photographed at Hamot Hospital. *From the* Erie Daily Times.

went to the cellar and got the machinist hammer. It was daylight. I then walked into my wife's bedroom. I stood beside my sleeping wife for a short while, holding the hammer, trying to get nerve enough to hit her on the head. I raised it three or four times, and then suddenly, I began hitting her on the head.

Weed paused, his eyes agglutinated to the ceiling. "She cried out, "Oh! My God!" But I didn't stop. I kept hitting her and hitting her. Then I began hitting David. David was silent. I then walked over to the crib where Charles was sleeping. When I hit him, he cried out, 'Oh, Daddy!' I just couldn't stop. I just kept hitting him and hitting him."

"You know the definition of sin?" Laub asked.

"Yes," Weed replied.

"You also know the difference between right and wrong?"

"Yes."

"Was your sin atoned?"

"No," Weed said, looking to Laub. "I committed another one."

"You know that you violated the law of God and man?"

"Yes, I do."

"You then attempted suicide to escape punishment of man?"

"Yes."

"You know one of the provisions of the Ten Commandments, 'Thou shall not kill'?"

"Yes."

"Do you think you would have been punished if you were killed by an automobile?"

"No. It would have continued in the next world," Weed said, turning his gaze back to the ceiling.

When pressed about the "scarlet sin" he committed, Weed refused to elaborate. When told that his son Charles, who was found alive, had succumbed to his wounds, Weed remained unfazed. When asked about the details preceding the murder, Weed spoke freely, his response later documented by Dr. Strimple:

About six weeks ago, the patient began to feel that he was no longer able to competently carry on his duties at the church or factory. This feeling was progressive, and as he "always talked matters over freely with God," presented the matter to him. The outcome was that God advised him to continue as usual. And as the patient refused, God would not forgive him. This climaxed a religious strife covering a two-year period. During that time, God had, many times, forgiven the patient for stealing small articles, namely nuts, screws, bolts, wire and pipe from the General Electric Company, and for continuing the practice of masturbation. The patient states that each of these three things played an equal part in his break with God, as the duties "patience was exhausted," because of the repetition of the practices, and forgiveness was no longer possible....About four weeks ago [on June 20, 1936] the devil first talked to him and advised him that his mental conflict would be abolished if he would run away from everything. On the next Sunday afternoon, he attempted this by going for a long walk, during which the devil constantly harassed him and urged him to commit suicide by throwing himself into a creek. Because he was afraid, the devil laughed, calling him "yellow," which further upset the patient.... During the following week, the patient spoke of his mental troubles to both his minister and his wife, telling them only that his mind was full of religious conflict. They promised to help him in this difficulty. Since the incident at the creek, the efforts of the devil to torment him increased daily—the voice telling him not to work, to commit suicide while at work, and on two occasions woke him up at night for this purpose. The patient's explanation for not completing the act was the lack of an effective means. As a reward for killing himself, the devil promised him relief from his worries and reinstatement into God's favor.

Regarding the events that occurred on the morning of July 18, 1936, Dr. Strimple recorded Weed's responses:

On July 18, 1936, the patient got up at 6:00 a.m. The devil appeared and repeated his suicidal command. The patient was again afraid to obey and was at a loss to know how his family would continue without a means of sustenence [sic]. The devil then told [him] the family would be better off in heaven and that God would forgive the patient for the murder of his family. With this promise in mind, he proceeded to murder his family and to commit suicide in order to join them.

When Weed was questioned by police, reporters and medical personnel, his mental responses were noted as being slow, deliberate and brief, with information obtained only after constant repetition. Not once did Samuel Weed show any change in emotion when discussing the murders.

Weed was asked by a reporter in the room if he was sorry for the murder. "I don't know," Weed shrugged. "There's no telling."

Despite Weed's confession, detectives remained puzzled.

By all accounts, Samuel Weed appeared to be a doting family man who loved his children and his wife, Irene. Weed had no past criminal record and often attended church with his family. Irene would sometimes teach Sunday school in the Nazarene Church, while Samuel served as the superintendent of the classes. He even sometimes stepped in to deliver sermons while the church pastor was away.

The night before the murder, members of the Nazarene Church prayed and sang hymns until 11:00 p.m. at the Weed home. Nothing out of the ordinary was noticed except for one moment when Samuel Weed was observed yelling, "Oh, God, help me! Oh, God, help me!" Weed was seen kissing his wife and children good night, taking the time to tuck his son David into bed with a small children's storybook. After the church members left, Weed went to bed.

The Weed family had lived at 1124 East Twentieth Street for seven years. Before living there, the Weed family had temporarily lived with Alice Chapin, Irene's mother, a former schoolteacher. And at the time of the incident, Samuel and Irene had been married for seven years.

Hamot Hospital. *From the Erie County Historical Society.*

As for the life insurance policies on Irene Weed and the two sons, police did not feel the murders were committed in an attempt to recoup the money from those policies.

By the evening of July 18, the services for Irene, David and Charles Weed had been announced. They would be held at the Edward C. Hanley and Sons Funeral Home in Erie. Reverend D.J. Blasdell of the Methodist church of Edinboro would officiate the services before their burial was to take place on July 21 at Wales Cemetery, located in Greene Township, Pennsylvania.

Many who spoke about the case believed that only an insane person would massacre his own family like Weed had.

District Attorney Graham disagreed. "There's a difference between medical and legal insanity," Graham told a reporter for the *Times.* "This man knew the difference between right and wrong. He said he did it and further showed it by trying to kill himself, as he explained, to escape the punishment of mankind and leave his fate to God."

The motive for the murders, according to City of Erie Police chief George Christoph, pointed to Weed's self-proclaimed "scarlet sin." "I am led to believe that there may be another woman or a girl in the case," Christoph mentioned to reporters. "What else could this 'scarlet sin' mean? I can see no real reason behind the slayings other than Weed may have felt remorseful about his relations with another woman or a girl."

Christoph also shrugged off suggestions that Weed was insane. "I would say that he is quite sane but somewhat of a religious fanatic. He talked cogently with us. He answered questions with a clear mind. The only thing he would not do was tell us about his 'scarlet sin.' Of course, he may break later on, but from the way the case stacks up now, I believe he'll carry the story of his 'scarlet sin' to the grave."

Just before noon on July 19, Robert Holmes, the police officer assigned to guard Samuel Weed, was sitting on the left edge of the bed reading a newspaper when Weed sat up and suddenly lunged at him, reaching for the pistol in his holster. The two became entangled.

A nurse, Claudia Bruckner, entered the room, and upon seeing the struggle, she screamed for help. Dr. Allen McGill, one of the interns who had tended to Weed the day prior, rushed to Weed's room and assisted Holmes. It was only after Holmes landed several punches against Weed's head that all three were able to secure him against the bed as other nurses arrived with a straitjacket.

Holmes later filed his report, detailing the event. "The man seemed to be resting, although he often raised his head from the pillow, and I didn't think much of that," Holmes said. "It's a good thing that he didn't get the gun, or I probably would not have been here to make this report. Weed meant business."

After Weed was restrained to his bed, he remained cooperative and showed no further signs of any "maniacal seizures or even of fits or convulsions," according to Dr. McGill.

As the investigation into the murder continued, County Detective LeRoy Search interviewed additional members of Weed's church and more neighbors. Despite the numerous interviews, however, Search could find nothing negative that was said about Samuel Weed. "This man has lived a quiet life and has been a Sunday school superintendent and apparently a normal citizen," Search later admitted.

Other avenues of the investigation included locating other relatives and inquiring about Weed's character and past activities. Detectives also looked at the possible angle Weed that had committed adultery, as some information indicated a potential mystery woman from Wesleyville.

Although police were not ruling out any possibilities at that point, District Attorney Graham admitted all rumors were merely presumptions at that point. As Graham's office began planning for trial in the upcoming September term of court, Samuel Weed's health improved, despite some pain in his head. As the investigation came to a close, authorities ordered additional monitoring of Weed to ensure he would not succeed in committing suicide.

The warden of the Erie County Jail, Matt Hess, also planned to enact a twenty-four-hour guard over Weed once he was transferred from Hamot Hospital. A reporter for the *Erie Dispatch Herald* interviewed Weed, asking what he intended to do when he appeared before a judge.

"I'm going to plead guilty to the murders," Weed said.

"That means you'll get the electric chair." the reporter added.

"I'm willing to die," Weed mumbled. "I don't want to live."

On July 20, 1936, almost five thousand men, women and children from all walks of life visited the funeral home as Irene, David and Charles Weed were laid out. Reporters from the *Times* noted that despite the extensive injuries Samuel Weed had inflicted on his family, efforts had been made to restore the features of the deceased.

Those who passed the open caskets agreed great care had been taken in presenting the bodies, with all three dressed in white. *Dispatch Herald* reporter Barbara Hawley was present for the funeral on the morning of July 20, 1936. As family members gathered in the adjoining rooms of the funeral home to wait for the service, Hawley noted a distinct silence matted against the sounds of a swelling organ in another room.

Hawley wrote that the three members of the Weed family appeared as though they were sleeping. Regarding Irene Weed, Hawley wrote, "On one of the woman's slender fingers was a narrow white gold wedding ring. In her thin hands was clasped a tiny, withering bouquet of roses. She had loved flowers. Her dress and the couch on which she lay were pale ashes of roses."

Hawley also wrote about David and Charles: "David, five, and Charles, her sons, in matching white sailor suits, white socks and strap slippers, each clasped a celluloid toy in chubby hands. Their peaceful faces, like hers, were unmarred."

Reverend Carl J. Lindeman of the Nazarene Mission Church and Reverend D.J. Blasdell, a Methodist minister from Edinboro, began the service with the first verses of Psalms 46 and 121, adding words of comfort as they stood before the three white coffins.

Following the service, Irene Weed's flower-covered coffin, followed by those of her sons, was led through a dressing room to the adjoining garage, where they were placed into two hearses. Irene Weed's two brothers, Cecil and Norman Chapin, along with two cousins, acted as pallbearers.

COMMON GRAVE CLAIMS WEED VICTIMS

The burials of Irene, David and Charles Weed in Wales Cemetery. *From the* Erie Daily Times.

A small cortege of vehicles, eleven in all, departed the funeral home for the Wales Cemetery. At the nearby intersection, small crowds of people solemnly looked on, paying their respects as the vehicles passed.

Arriving at the cemetery, reporter Barbara Hawley wrote:

> *Through the neighborhood where Irene Wed played when a girl, over tree-lined roads and under sunny skies, they carried her "home" again, to lie in Wales Cemetery near the small frame church which she had attended in her youth, surrounded by the trees which have caused Wales to be described as*

the prettiest small cemetery in Pennsylvania....Cameras clicked as the two smaller caskets, David on her left and Charles on her right, were lowered into the wide open grave beside her, and again when a gasping breath was wrenched from the gray-haired woman who stood at their feet as the solemn words, "Earth to earth," were intoned....The gray-haired woman, mother and grandmother of the three now deep in their concrete crypts, sobbed audibly as she buried her head on the shoulder of a black-clad woman beside her, and turned away. The busy cameras clicked again.

Country folk and family of the deceased gathered around the graves and spoke with Hawley, expressing their opinions about the ordeal. "We love Sam still. We know he wasn't responsible!" someone yelled as others murmured in agreement. "He needs help."

"It's the first victims of a murder we've buried in the cemetery since it was opened in 1840," mentioned another.

As Irene Weed's family gathered in prayer on the grounds of the Wales Cemetery that morning, Samuel Weed's family hired the service of local attorney Edward G. Petrillo.

In 1936, Edward G. Petrillo was a well-known local attorney among Erie's Italian community. Born in Naples, Italy, on November 7, 1885, Petrillo was an athlete at the Royal University of Naples. After graduating from the Royal University of Naples, Italy, with a degree in diplomacy and a doctorate of law, he and his wife immigrated to America in 1910, becoming American citizens within two years of their arrival in Erie, Pennsylvania.

Petrillo quickly mastered English and studied law under the sponsorship of local attorney Monroe J. Echols. In the spring of 1918, Petrillo took his exams in Philadelphia and passed the bar exam on his first attempt. Serving during World War I, Petrillo later became a specialist in both civil and criminal cases, and he became an expert on international and immigration laws and served in the state capital of Harrisburg as a deputy attorney general until 1932.

After announcing he would represent Samuel Weed, Petrillo informed reporters he would ask permission of the court for Weed to plead guilty by reason of insanity, guaranteeing his removal to an institution instead of facing the electric chair.

The first step, Petrillo added, would be to have doctors examine Weed and prove beyond all reasonable doubt that he was insane at the time of the murders. Petrillo confirmed that he had enlisted the assistance of Dr. Ira B. Darling of the Warren State Hospital and Dr. J.J. O'Donnell of Erie, along with a third doctor from Pittsburgh. "There is no question in my mind that

Downtown Erie, looking north. Note the Boston Store to the left. *From the Erie County Historical Society.*

Weed is insane," Petrillo said. "This man was physically sick and worrying over financial matters and other difficulties until his mind suddenly gave way."

The Erie County District Attorney's Office planned to fight any attempt to save Samuel Weed from his date with the electric chair. "We are still convinced this killer is sane, and we will use every effort to have him executed," Assistant District Attorney Burton R. Laub said, repeating his statement from the days previous. "Unless we know Weed will be sent to the chair when he pleads guilty, we will continue to try to bring him to trial. We are confident any jury selected will decide he is guilty of murder in the first degree."

By Thursday, July 23, 1936, final preparations were already underway for Weed's removal to the Erie County Jail. Weed remained restrained in a straitjacket but was continuing to improve, both mentally and physically.

As for defense attorney Edward G. Petrillo and Assistant District Attorney Burton R. Laub, both agreed to engage a commission of three doctors to examine Weed. A brief report in the press that stated Weed had suffered a hemorrhage and taken a turn for the worse was later proven false by Hamot Hospital officials.

District Attorney Graham decided to propose to Edward Petrillo that three prominent mental experts be employed by the commonwealth and that the defense could also proceed with examining Weed, confirming their decisions would be determined as final in the case.

"He's in a state of lethargy. He has a pulse that reaches 130 at times and refuses to talk when police are around. I have studied him closely and am convinced he is a mental case," Dr. James Strimple added when asked by the *Times* about his thoughts on Weed's sanity. "I asked him yesterday if he realized what he did and why he did it, and he replied with a fixed stare, 'It was the devil in me.'"

Police officers assigned to guard Weed also commented on Weed's mental state. Officer Edward Alberstadt remarked that Weed told him, "What's the difference? There's an end to all this." Officer Andrew Vamos remarked Weed was consistently in a state of extreme nervousness and that he "keeps pounding his fists on the bed."

Dr. Charles Leone, the acting coroner, announced on July 25 that he would gather witnesses and call for an inquest into the murder to be held on Tuesday, July 28, at the Erie County Courthouse. Reports leaked to the media indicated some of the doctors who examined Weed were of the opinion that he was in fact insane, throwing doubt on the fact that he would be tried in the court of common pleas in Erie.

On Tuesday, July 28, 1936, a coroner's inquest into the murders of Irene, David and Charles Weed concluded with the jury returning the verdict that Samuel Weed was responsible for their murders. Following the inquest, which lasted only twenty minutes, defense attorney Petrillo filed a petition to ask for the appointment of a guardian in an attempt to have Samuel Weed officially declared incompetent for trial.

Petrillo justified his petition by stating that one of the doctors who had already examined Weed at Hamot Hospital felt that he was insane and would declare so in a report that was to be released and filed later. But he refused to reveal the doctor's name when asked.

District Attorney Graham also revealed to reporters that there was a growing dispute over the collection of life insurance money for Irene, David and Charles Weed.

Petrillo vehemently argued against Graham's implications, stating he was acting on behalf of Samuel Weed. In Pennsylvania in 1936, state law stated no killer may benefit from a homicidal act; however, the statute did not apply to those ruled insane. Because Weed was insane, Petrillo argued he was not guilty in accordance with Pennsylvania state law and, therefore, was legally allowed to collect on the life insurance policies for his wife and children.

Not persuaded by Petrillo's arguments, Graham claimed Weed knew what he was doing at the time of the murders and was still considered legally sane.

When asked again to turn over the insurance policies, Graham refused, saying he would instead turn them over to Robert Hanley, the administrator of Irene Weed's estate. Edward Petrillo prepared his petition and placed it before Judge William E. Hirt, asking for a hearing be held prior to September.

Hirt presented a wry smile as he looked at the petition. "Is this Weed the man who is accused of murder?" Judge Hirt asked.

Petrillo informed Judge Hirt that he was correct.

"I congratulate you upon your technique, Mr. Petrillo, but this hearing will not be held until after the man's trial in September. I'll fix the first Monday in October as the date for hearing," Judge Hirt said.

Despite the back-and-forth wrangling between the defense and prosecution, some considerable ground was gained when District Attorney Graham suggested the possible aid of Pennsylvania attorney general Charles J. Margiotti in getting psychiatrists to examine Samuel Weed. Margiotti, a famed criminal lawyer, could provide considerable aid in choosing the experts needed to determine Weed's mental competency, Graham added.

When presented with Graham's suggestions, Petrillo said he would confer further with Graham in an attempt to reach an agreement on a selection of psychiatrists. "Everything hinges on the report the alienists will make, and we consequently want the finest men available to conduct the examination," Graham said to reporters on July 30, 1936.

On July 31, 1936, after being hospitalized for thirteen days, Samuel Weed was discharged from Hamot Hospital into the custody of the City of Erie Police Department. Drs. McGill and Strimple wrote the following in Weed's treatment and progress record: "July 31: Discharge today. General condition good. Head wound good. No evidence recently of nervous attacks—mentally more alert and willing to talk more as then on admission. Discharge to custody of city police."

Following his release, Samuel Weed was brought before Alderman William Schabacker on three separate charges of murder. When arraigned before Schabacker, Weed was asked how he wanted to plead. "I'm the one who did it." Weed responded.

Following his guilty plea, a preliminary hearing was set for August 7 at 2:00 p.m. Samuel Weed had just begun the fight for his right to end his life.

CURSE OF THE SCARLET SIN

On August 7, 1936, Samuel Weed's preliminary hearing took place at the office of Alderman William Schabacker. After entering Schabacker's office, Weed was turned over by Warden Matt Hess to Officers Jake Zimmer and Charles Detzel. Both Assistant District Attorney Burton R. Laub and Weed's defense attorney Edward Petrillo argued back and forth, with Laub insisting the hearing be continued and Petrillo asking for the hearing to be waived.

Petrillo told Schabacker that two of his witnesses were not present, and he asked for the hearing to be postponed pending the outcome of a sanity test Weed was to be given, claiming he intended to prove Weed was insane when he committed the murders. Laub argued the question of sanity had no bearing on the case based on the fact that the preliminary hearing was to determine evidence in the case.

Alderman Schabacker ultimately ruled the hearing would continue.

Petrillo responding by waiving the hearing, explaining he would not dispute the facts in the case. This prompted an objection from Laub before Alderman Schabacker, who was already irritated, to again advise Petrillo the hearing would continue. "I'll plead the defendant, who is silent, not guilty to the three separate charges of murder," Laub continued.

With the charges already read to Weed, Schabacker called the first witness in what would culminate to ninety minutes of testimony that afternoon. The first witnesses called were reporters Ralph "Bat" Humble and Eugene Jana, who were the first to arrive at Weeds' home following the call made to dispatch.

Laub showed photographs of Samuel Weed's murdered family as a description of the gruesome crime scene was explained in graphic detail.

Patrolman Carl Malinowski, who arrested Weed, provided testimony, along with Detective Sergeant George Barber. Deputy Coroner Dr. Charles Leon, who performed the autopsies on the three victims, testified all three had suffered multiple skull fractures which resulted in death.

Throughout the proceeding, Weed was silent, his hands folded on his lap and head bowed. He was seated between his defense attorney and prosecutor. He weighed around one hundred pounds, and newspaper reporters remarked he looked healthier.

"How do you feel?" a reporter asked Weed.

Weed remained silent, only nodding his head.

Following the hearing, Schabacker ordered Weed bound over for the upcoming September grand jury, and then he was escorted back to the Erie County Jail.

District Attorney Mortimer Graham, speaking to the public following the hearing, cemented his plans to do everything necessary to ensure that Samuel Weed would sit in the electric chair, disputing that Weed was mentally insane when committing the murders by pointing to discussions Weed had with Chief Christoph at Hamot Hospital, in which he confirmed he knew right from wrong when he committed the crime.

By August 11, 1936, Graham had started to prepare for trial, along with his staff of assistants, reexamining the evidence that was to go before the September grand jury. If Weed stood trial and was found guilty of first-degree murder, it would be the first time since 1929 a convicted criminal from Erie went to the electric chair.

By mid-August, however, Graham's office had yet to hire any psychiatrists to determine whether Samuel Weed was sane at the time of the murder. Graham soon traveled to Philadelphia, where he spoke to two of the country's most well-known mental health experts, Dr. Charles W. Burr and Dr. Daniel J. McCarthy. Dr. Burr was considered one of the top authorities on criminal insanity, and Dr. McCarthy, who was also an attorney, specialized in medical jurisprudence in relation to criminal insanity and was the author of several books on the subject.

Graham's meeting in Philadelphia would shock those in Erie who were waiting for an impending trial.

At a scheduled press conference on August 18, Graham advised that the doctors had studied Weed's clinical data and his life from the time he was born until present, along with the details of the crime, and informed Graham that Weed suffered from a "well defined type of insanity, commonly known as religious mania."

Weed, the doctors added, was a danger to society and should be incarcerated for the rest of his life. "In view of the report, we do not feel justified in bringing Weed to trial," Graham continued. "We will ask the court to either confine him in Warren State Hospital for general observation or order him direct to Fairview Hospital for the Criminally Insane."

When asked why he had suddenly reversed course on trying Weed, Graham hesitated for a moment before carefully crafting his response. "Until I talked to the two doctors, I had believed Weed legally sane. I preferred to have the best men available make the final ruling. Weed, as a result of that decision, will not be prosecuted for the three murders."

This was not to say that those who committed homicide in Erie County and were ruled mentally incompetent could not regain their sanity in the future. Harold Martish, who shot and killed Robert McKee at a gas station near

Girard on January 4, 1935, was sent to Fairview State Hospital and released as a sane individual in 1935, but he was never prosecuted for the crime.

On Thursday, August 20, 1936, Erie County judge Miles B. Kitts was asked by the district attorney's office to grant a committal order that would send Samuel Weed to the Fairview State Hospital for the Criminally Insane. Under state law, this would allow the court to name its own physicians to examine Weed and issue a report. Although Drs. Burr and McCarthy had already ruled Weed insane at the time of the crime, the procedure was more a matter of routine.

Judge Kitts appointed Drs. Felix S. Shubert and Edward H. Drozeski on April 20 to give Samuel Weed a sanity test. Upon the completion of their report, should Shubert and Drozeski agree that Weed was insane, it would clear the way for an order to commit him to either the Warren State Hospital or Fairview Hospital for the Criminally Insane.

On August 22, 1936, Shubert and Drozeski submitted their report after examining Weed and confirmed he suffered from religious mania. They agreed with the prior assessments of insanity. "Careful mental examination and study of his medical history elicited the fact that he has been definitely insane since the first week in June, having continued and repeated hallucinations of a mandatory type from the devil of a suicidal and homicidal nature," the report stated. "Further, he has been much perturbed and upset emotionally by a religious strife for a period of two years, suggesting mental diseases dating back that far."

With the report submitted to Judge Kitts, plans were submitted to have Weed removed from the county jail the following week.

The Weed case, however, continued to captivate and cause concern in Erie, with one person, writing under the pseudonym "A Business Woman" in a letter to the editor of the *Erie Daily Times* on August 24, stating: "No one ever seems to ask the questions an intelligent man asks: What is their mental capacity? Were they normal, sane, responsible? Some day we may wake up and stick a psychologist into our district attorney's office."

Samuel Weed was transported to the Fairview State Hospital on August 29, 1936. For the greater length of the car ride to the state hospital, the trip was uneventful. But when they reached Carbondale, Pennsylvania, the vehicle was forced from the road and nearly turned over. "It's too bad we were not all killed," Weed remarked to the two men who were accompanying him in the back seat.

When Erie County sheriff Dell Darling and Deputy Fred Struchen delivered Weed to the state hospital in Fairview, Weed had nothing to say.

On September 22, 1936, local Erie attorney Edward E. Petrillo was appointed by Erie County judge William E. Hirt as guardian of the affairs for Samuel Weed, following a petition by Weed's siblings asking for a guardian to be appointed, as Weed was no longer capable of administering his own affairs.

Weed's affairs consisted of maintaining the family home on East Twentieth Street, still under mortgage, along with several other items he owned, a small amount of money he had and a life insurance policy he had taken out on himself. The appointment of Petrillo to oversee Weed's affairs caused scorn from the public, as Weed, who clearly murdered his wife and children, could still profit from the crime, even if he was never released. "No attempt will ever be made to free him unless doctors at the institution decide he has become sane," Petrillo assured reporters.

Following his assignment as Weed's guardianship, Petrillo filed three suits, aggregating $2,400 against local undertaker Robert E. Hanley on Tuesday, September 29, 1935. The suits represented the sum paid to Hanley as administrator of the estates of Weed's wife and two sons regarding their life insurance policies.

Petrillo argued that Weed was entitled to the money, claiming a portion of it would be needed for Weed's retirement obligations. In agreement with Petrillo, Hanley responded with a request for the local courts to determine who should be in charge of the insurance money.

On Thursday, November 5, 1936, Judge William E. Hirt decided Weed was entitled to the insurance payments for the deaths of his wife and sons, basing his decision on the proposition of law that Weed had been found not guilty of felonious homicide by reason of insanity. Petrillo was paid the full amounts of the insurance policies, less than the cost of funeral expenses: $910 for the life of Irene Weed, $32.80 for the life of Charles Weed and $112.25 for the life of David Weed.

JUSTICE NEVER SERVED

When Erie County deputy sheriff Harry Darling was at Fairview State Hospital in September 1937 for business, he was informed by officials there that Weed was declared cured and that a recommendation for his release would follow shortly. This news surprised Darling, who spoke to Weed himself. Darling later told reporters he believed Weed was "as normal now as any other man."

A little over a year after the murders, the religious mania that mysteriously drove Weed to commit murder had vanished. The *Erie Daily Times* broke the news that Weed would go free the following day, September 29, 1937, with the headline: "ERIE SLAYER OF WIFE, 2 KIDDIES TO GO FREE."

Those in Erie who followed the sensational crime hoped that justice would finally be served, with Weed being ordered to stand trial for the murders.

That brief hope, however, was extinguished by District Attorney Mortimer E. Graham, who confirmed that since all the mental experts involved in the case at the time had agreed Weed was mentally insane when the murders occurred, he was barred from future prosecution in the case.

Despite the news reports, however, Weed remained an inmate at the Fairview State Hospital.

Toward the end of 1942, Samuel Weed, still confined at Fairview State Hospital, was provided "ground parole," which allowed him greater freedom on the premises of the state hospital and limited both his supervision and confinement. However, it stopped short of releasing him to the general public.

On Tuesday, March 30, 1943, Erie County judge Miles B. Kitts signed a discharge order for Samuel Weed to be released from the Fairview State Hospital. Weed was to be returned by Erie County sheriff Fred Lamberton to the Erie County Jail following his release.

Dr. John Rutherford of Fairview State Hospital corresponded with Judge Kitts, indicating he felt Weed no longer needed custodial care or treatment and recommending his discharge. District Attorney Burton R. Laub would again confirm the legalities surrounding the case, saying the case would never be presented before a courtroom.

Upon his return on April 15, 1943, Weed had little to say about the murders except that they felt like a dream to him. When he was told he may have to remain in the jail for a few more days until his release, Weed shrugged and noted that he had already been in custody for so long that a few more days would not matter.

Samuel Weed, Lamberton remarked to reporters, had an excellent record while incarcerated at the Fairview State Hospital and that his record was such that he was allowed to leave the institution at various times, during which he conducted himself in an appropriate manner. As expected, Edward E. Petrillo filed and presented the writ for habeas corpus before Judge Kitts, and after conferring with District Attorney Laub, the writ was approved on the afternoon of April 16.

Samuel Weed quietly walked out of the Erie County Jail at the age of forty-seven and disappeared from the area, eventually moving out of the state to Westfield, New York, to stay with one of his sisters.

On the afternoon of Thursday, January 26, 1950, after failing to report downstairs for lunch when called, C. Weed was found by his nephew hanging from a high bed post in the upstairs bedroom of his sister's home on Ogden Road in Westfield, New York. He had tied roughly four or five pieces of cord together and fashioned one end around the bedpost and the other around his neck.

Samuel Weed was later interred in Westfield Cemetery, located in Westfield, New York.

Wales Cemetery, the final resting place of Irene Weed and her two sons, David and Charles, is nestled on the outskirts of the City of Erie, tucked into the rolling hillsides and valleys of the county, far away from the noise and bustle of the big city.

As you make your way to the rear of the cemetery, passing through haphazard rows of dilapidated and chipped tombstones, you can find the graves of Irene, David and Charles Weed situated on a slight rise of land overlooking farmlands and abundant wood lots. Birds chirp against the faint breeze, and the afternoon sun there brings with it serene peace, which was denied to Irene Weed and her sons on July 18, 1936.

After more than fifty years of service as an attorney-at-law, Edward E. Petrillo was recognized and admired not only for his professional competence but also for his conduct in his professional and personal life. In 1966, Petrillo was awarded knighthood by the Italian government for his work on behalf of newly arrived Italian immigrants in the United States, and in 1969, he was honored by the Erie County Bar Association as chancellor of the bar. While vacationing in Fort Lauderdale, Florida, in February 1969, Petrillo suffered from a combination of a stroke and an aneurysm and later died at the age of eighty-four. Petrillo posthumously received accolades from Erie City Council members in tribute to his memory.

The Weed home, which stood at 2114 East Twentieth Street, stood until June 2013, when it was razed to the ground. As of November 2022, only the foundation of the home and its detached garage remain.

Fairview State Hospital, which operated as Pennsylvania's only institution for the criminally insane, closed in 1995 and has since been repurposed as a state correctional facility, SCI Waymart.

The Erie County Courthouse's files of the court of oyer and terminer at the Erie County Historical Society hold only several pieces of paper within the case file of the *Commonwealth of Pennsylvania v. Samuel C. Weed*, the most important being paperwork related to Weed's admission to Hamot Hospital

A present-day view of 2114 East Twentieth Street. *Author's collection.*

The corner of Franklin Avenue and Buffalo Road, where Samuel Weed was arrested. *Author's collection.*

The graves of Irene, David and Charles Weed in Wales Cemetery. *Author's collection.*

following his attempted suicide. Other documents, such as the preliminary hearing transcript, have long since disappeared.

Seventy-three years after Samuel Weed's suicide, however, the scarlet sin case—Erie's first mass murder—continues to baffle those who study its details. It leaves one haunting question: what was Samuel Weed's scarlet sin?

BIBLIOGRAPHY

Commonwealth of Pennsylvania v. Carl Penetzke, John Costa and Earl McBride. Erie County Court of Common Pleas. No. 35. May 1909.

Commonwealth of Pennsylvania v. Ferdinand Fischer. Erie County Court of Common Pleas. No. 76. September 1908.

Commonwealth of Pennsylvania v. John Trevison. Erie County Court of Common Pleas. Nos. 7 and 8. September 1929.

Commonwealth of Pennsylvania v. Leoni Massi. Erie County Court of Common Pleas. No. 26. May 1926.

Commonwealth of Pennsylvania v. Samuel C. Weed. Erie County Court of Common Pleas. Nos. 1, 2, and 3. September 1936.

Dayton Daily News. February 15, 1926.

Dayton Herald. July 8, 1926.

Democrat and Chronicle. October 14, 1914.

Erie County Bar Association. *Memoirs of the Erie County, Pennsylvania, BENCH and BAR*. Vol. 2. 1ˢᵗ ed. Erie, PA: Erie County Bar Foundation, 2000.

Erie Daily Times. October 30, 1890; November 8, 1890; September 2, 1891; October 27, 1892; September 28, 1894; October 2, 1894; June 9, 1900; September 3, 1902; February 28, 1905; March 1, 1905; February 12, 1907; February 28, 1908; March 12, 1908; September 11, 1908; September 12, 1908; September 14, 1908; September 15, 1908; September 16, 1908; September 18, 1908; September 25, 1908; September 26, 1908; November 11, 1908; November 12, 1908; November 17, 1908; November 19, 1908; April 9, 1909; April 10, 1909; April 12, 1909; May 25, 1909; June 21, 1909; June 22, 1909; June 29, 1909; August 23, 1909; January 10, 1910;

January 11, 1910; January 12, 1910; January 13, 1910; February 8, 1910; March 5, 1910; March 7, 1910; May 4, 1910; May 5, 1910; February 4, 1919; February 20, 1919; April 7, 1921; April 8, 1921; April 9, 1921; April 16, 1921; May 3, 1921; May 12, 1925; July 7, 1925; October 7, 1925; December 28, 1925; December 30, 1925; January 1, 1926; January 2, 1926; January 5, 1926; January 7, 1926; January 15, 1926; January 18, 1926; January 20, 1926; January 21, 1926; January 23, 1926; January 25, 1926; January 26, 1926; January 27, 1926; January 30, 1926; February 1, 1926; February 2, 1926; February 3, 1926; February 4, 1926; March 1, 1926; March 2, 1926; April 7, 1926; April 8, 1926; April 13, 1926; May 17, 1926; May 22, 1926; December 13, 1926; December 21, 1926; December 22, 1926; December 23, 1926; January 11, 1927; January 12, 1927; January 24, 1927; September 2, 1927; September 5, 1927; September 6, 1927; September 7, 1927; September 15, 1927; September 20, 1927; September 30, 1927; October 11, 1927; October 15, 1927; October 17, 1927; October 18, 1927; November 8, 1927; November 11, 1927; November 14, 1927; November 17, 1927; November 21, 1927; November 26, 1927; December 6, 1927; December 7, 1927; January 2, 1928; January 17, 1928; February 16, 1928; May 21, 1928; May 22, 1928; May 23, 1928; May 24, 1928; May 25, 1928; June 2, 1928; June 7, 1928; June 11, 1928; August 11, 1928; September 17, 1928; September 18, 1928; September 21, 1928; September 19, 1928; September 24, 1928; May 15, 1929; March 19, 1931; March 20, 1931; March 23, 1931; March 24, 1931; March 25, 1931; March 26, 1931; March 27, 1931; March 31, 1931; April 1, 1931; April 2, 1931; April 18, 1931; April 25, 1931; April 25, 1931; April 29, 1931; April 30, 1931; May 1, 1931; May 11, 1931; May 12, 1931; May 13, 1931; May 15, 1931; May 16, 1931; May 18, 1931; May 22, 1931; May 23, 1931; August 18, 1932; November 10, 1932; June 6, 1933; October 3, 1933; October 17, 1933; February 13, 1934; February 27, 1934; August 29, 1934; January 1, 1935; January 29, 1935; February 4, 1935; February 22, 1935; September 13, 1935; December 17, 1935; December 23, 1935; July 18, 1936; July 20, 1936; July 23, 1936; July 25, 1936; July 28, 1936; July 30, 1936; July 31, 1936; August 8, 1936; August 14, 1936; August 18, 1936; August 19, 1936; August 22, 1936; August 24, 1936; August 25, 1936; August 31, 1936; September 22, 1936; September 29, 1936; October 6, 1936; November 5, 1936; September 29, 1937; March 30, 1943; April 16, 1943; January 27, 1950; February 20, 1956; June 3, 1968; June 20, 1971; December 4, 1972; October 31, 1974; September 23, 1975; September 26, 1975.

Erie Dispatch. March 1, 1908; September 11, 1908; September 16, 1908; November 17, 1908; November 18, 1908; April 13, 1909; December 30, 1925; January 2, 1926; January 4, 1926; January 5, 1926; January 14, 1926; January 19, 1926; January 24, 1926; January 26, 1926; January 27, 1926; January 31, 1926; February 3, 1926; February 9, 1926; September 2, 1927; March 19, 1931; March 20, 1931; March 21, 1931; March 22, 1931; July 18, 1936; July 20, 1936; July 21, 1936; July 22, 1936.

Erie Evening Herald. February 28, 1908; February 29, 1908; March 2, 1908.

Erie Morning News. March 4, 1974.

Greeneville Sun. November 4, 1948.

Hunt, Thomas P., and Michael A. Tona. "Daniel Sansanese, Sr. (May 28, 1908–Nov. 1, 1975)." In *DiCarlo: Buffalo's First Family of Crime*. Research Triangle, NC: Lulu.com, 2013.

Oldfield, William, and Victoria Bruce. *Inspector Oldfield and the Black Hand Society: America's Original Gangsters and the U.S. Postal Detective Who Brought Them to Justice*. New York: Touchstone, 2018.

Rust, Albert E. *History of Erie County Electric Company*. Erie, PA: A-K-D Printing Company, 1931.

Walling, Emory A. (judge). *Memoirs of the Erie County Pennsylvania Bench and Bar*. Erie, PA: Press of the Erie Printing Company, 1928.

Warren Times Mirror. June 24, 1909.

Webb, Clifford. "Non-Payment." *Illustrated Detective Magazine*, March 1932.

ABOUT THE AUTHOR

*J*ustin Dombrowski has spent over sixteen years studying history within Erie County, Pennsylvania, specializing in Erie's criminal and legal historical records. A native of Erie, Pennsylvania, he is an alumnus of Mercyhurst University and can usually be found searching for his next historical adventure. This is his third book with The History Press. He resides in Erie, Pennsylvania.